OUR LADY SPEAKS

FROM MEDJUGORJE

Arranged According to Subject Matter

by
Andrew Jerome Yeung

OUR LADY SPEAKS

FROM MEDJUGORJE

Arranged According to Subject Matter

by Andrew Jerome Yeung

Third Edition

The Ave Maria Centre of Peace
P.O. Box 489, Station U
Toronto, Ontario, M8Z 5Y8
Canada

National Library of Canada Cataloguing in Publication Data

Main entry under title:
    Our Lady speaks from Medjugorje

3rd ed.
ISBN 0-9688426-0-7

    1. Mary, Blessed Virgin, Saint --Apparitions and miracles --Bosnia and Hercegovina --Medjugorje. I. Yeung, Andrew Jerome, 1938- II. Ave Maria Centre of Peace.

BT660.M44087 2002   232'.91'7'0949742   C2002-901024-1

Printed and bound in Canada
by the Ave Maria Centre of Peace

The painting on the front cover, *IN GOD'S HANDS*, is by Ljubo Jovanovic, and is used here by his personal permission.

FOREWORD

By Cathy Nolan

"Today as never before I invite you to live my messages and to put them into practice in your life" (03/25/92).

For more than twenty years, Our Lady has been giving us messages **"as it has never been done in history from the beginning of the world"** (04/04/85). Each of her messages has meaning for the time it is given, but also contains wisdom from the Queen of Heaven worthy of our continued attention. The question for me has always been, how can I study the messages and keep them alive in my heart? There are so many!

When I received *Our Lady Speaks from Medjugorje* in the mail, I got my answer. Here, in one small book, are the main messages arranged by topic. What has Our Lady said about prayer, about fasting, about the cross, about heaven? I can find the basic messages that treat the subject grouped together.

Our Lady said, **"I invite all of you to have more trust in me and to live my messages more deeply. I am with you and I intercede before God for you, but I also wait for your hearts to open up to my messages"** (05/25/94). I find that when I read and pray over a group of messages on a certain topic, I am filled with peace, and a new sense of understanding comes to me. Her words are pure and true. There is a powerful grace for

i

conversion attached to her messages. How wonderful it is to have them presented in this simple and useful way.

My husband, Denis, and I pray the Rosary weekly with a group of college students. Often we choose a topic from the book and read a message before each Hail Mary. The messages penetrate deeply into our hearts during those decades. Our Lady's words are channels of grace. Like dew in the desert they bring new life to our souls. Her words come alive in our hearts when we pray the Rosary in this way!

Our Lady's messages are a treasure to be cherished. They are a school of holiness, a strong gift of encouragement, and a tender caress of the most loving of mothers. We who have been so blessed by them now have a way to keep them close to us, deep in our hearts. "**Soon a time will come when you will lament for these messages**" (08/25/97). We still have time to respond.

Thank you, Andrew, for this marvellous little book that has made Our Lady's messages part of our daily life!

St. James' Church in Medjugorje

PREFACE

Since 1981, six Croatian youths in the village of Medjugorje, Bosnia-Herzegovina, have been asserting that they see the Blessed Virgin Mary and that they receive messages from her. For millions of people all over the world these extraordinary events, together with the heavenly instructions, have become a source of renewal within their Christian lives. The messages are in complete harmony with the Gospel and with Catholic tradition.

Although the Church's position on the occurrences is, at this stage, only one of watchful attention and investigation, unofficial pilgrimages to Medjugorje are neither prohibited nor discouraged. On the contrary, the Church acknowledges this village to be a sanctuary of prayer, and oversees the liturgical-pastoral services offered at the site.

Through Medjugorje, numerous Christians and non-Christians have found their way to God, to one another, and to the Church; this is what most characterizes Medjugorje, described by someone as "a place where it is very easy to turn to God and to start a new spiritual life." A large number of visitors have experienced conversion and various forms of healing.

The archbishop of Vienna, now His Eminence Christoph Cardinal Schoenborn, stated, "Personally, I have not been to Medjugorje, but in a certain way I have been there many times through the people I have met and the people I know. And in their lives I am seeing good fruit. I would be lying if I said this fruit did not exist. This fruit is concrete and visible, and I can see in our diocese and in many other places graces of conversion, graces of a supernatural life of faith, graces of joy, graces of vocations, of healings, of people returning to the Sacraments – to confession. All this is not misleading. Therefore, as far as I am concerned, as a bishop, I can see the fruit. If we had to judge the tree by its fruit, as Jesus recommended, I must say that the tree is fruitful."

In fact, Cardinal Schoenborn often tells his bishops and priests openly that 50% of the seminarians of his diocese have chosen this path thanks to Medjugorje, which was the place of their conversion or of their call to the priesthood.

The Cardinal's assertion about the return to the Sacraments can be partially attested to by the large number of communicants and confessions at Medjugorje. There are at least six Masses each day, and during the summer months, each one is attended by wall-to-wall pilgrims, more than what you see on Sundays in most churches in the rest of the world. Annually, the number of communion hosts used far exceeds one million. As well, there are 6 confessionals inside the church and a row of 25 more outside. Dozens of extra stations are set up around the grounds on big feast-days. The queues are long.

The editor of this book has travelled to Medjugorje more than 20 times. He is one of those for whom this hamlet became a second home. Staying there for several weeks on some occasions, Andrew witnessed and personally experienced the intense response to Our Lady's call in the surroundings in which they were given. He learned to speak a little Croatian, and made many friends among the parishioners, the visionaries and the pilgrims.

The seven books he has written have all been influenced by the Queen of Peace in one form or another.

I consider Andrew's book a very precious contribution to understanding the communications of Our Lady. Putting the more important subjects in alphabetical order, he helps us find an easy entrance to the riches of the wonderful guidance given by our loving Mother. On the one hand, for those who do not know them or who reject them purely out of ignorance, it gives a quick and clear view of what Mary is saying. On the other hand, for those who do know them and want to live them more fully, this systematic manual will be helpful in their meditations and in the revitalization of their faith.

I hope this work fulfills the author's wish of bringing to the reader the immense joy of becoming a better Christian. I hope it will serve as an inspiration for all to come closer to God, and to learn to pray and offer up their lives for the conversion of sinners and unbelievers. I hope also that priests and deacons will find in it valuable reminders for their preaching, counselling, and proclamation of the Gospel of Jesus Christ.

Marija Stelzer-Dugandzic
Native of Medjugorje. Close friend of the visionaries. Graduate of the prestigious Pontifical Gregorian University in Rome. Licentiate in Pastoral Theology from the University of Vienna. Author of *OUR LADY SPEAKS AS A MOTHER* - Textual Analysis and Theology of the Messages (Gebetsaktion – Medjugorje, Vienna).

TABLE OF CONTENTS

T O P I C S

4

INTRODUCTION

Background

The Blessed Virgin Mary first appeared in Medjugorje on June 24, 1981, to Ivanka Ivankovic and Mirjana Dragicevic; the two girls ran away. The next day she came to them again; Vicka Ivankovic, Ivan Dragicevic, Marija Pavlovic and Jakov Colo were also present. This second afternoon all six stayed to watch, listen and ask questions. At that time, Jakov was 10 years old while the others were just past their mid-teens. Since then Our Lady has been conveying messages to them on a regular basis. This manual contains a portion of the more important teachings. The entries include some additional information imparted to Jelena Vasilj by way of inner locutions.

The messages are not primarily forecasts about future events. Most of them are directions for living a solid spiritual life, directions which are pertinent in every age, no matter on what date they were initially given. Our Lady appeals especially for peace, reconciliation, conversion, prayer, strong faith, fasting and penance.

Critics

Opponents of Medjugorje like to justify their stance by arguing that there is no need for heavenly visitations, that Revelation was completed on the death of the last Apostle, that it is enough for a Christian to be guided by Sacred Scripture and the Church. That may be so, but we beg them to open their eyes and look around. How many people do they see reading Sacred Scripture? How many heed what is written in them? How many are faithful to

5

all the tenets of the Church? Our Lady has never said she came to announce a new set of revelations; she is here precisely to exhort her children to live what the Bible and the Catholic Church teaches!

"Look around you, dear children, and you will see how greatly sin has dominated the world," she said on September 13th, 1984. And again on October 8th, 1984, "The world is immersed in a great moral decay." Many of her children give in readily to sin; they ignore God; they live like pagans. Can a loving Mother stand by and do nothing? In the Spring of 1982 she had stated, "It is necessary to awaken the faith which is a gift from God. If it were called for, I would appear in every home."

Pope John Paul II on Medjugorje

From the Internet site officially sponsored by the Franciscan priests, one can read some of the documented remarks made by His Holiness.

To Bishop Pavol Hnilica (1984): *"Medjugorje is the continuation of Fatima."*

To the Medjugorje visionary Mirjana Dragicevic (1987): *"If I were not the Pope I would already be in Medjugorje confessing."*

To Bishop Maurillo Kreiger of Brazil (1988): *"Medjugorje, Medjugorje, it is the spiritual heart of the world."*

To a group of doctors in Italy (1989): *"Yes, today the world has lost its sense of the supernatural. In Medjugorje, many seek and rediscover it in prayer, fasting and confession."*

To Archbishop Angelo Kim, President of the Korean Bishops' Conference, in reply to his compliment to the

Pope, "Father, thanks to you, Poland was able to liberate itself from Communism" (1990): *"No, this is not my merit. This is the work of the Blessed Virgin Mary, as she had predicted in Fatima and in Medjugorje."*

To Fr. Jozo Zovko (1992): *"Busy yourself with Medjugorje, look after Medjugorje, don't tire. Persevere, be strong, I am with you. Watch over, follow, Medjugorje."*

To Archbishop Felipe Santiago Bentez of Paraguay (1994): *"Approve all that is related to Medjugorje."*

To Bishop Robert Cavallero of Chiavari, in answer to his question to the Holy Father whether he believed in Medjugorje (1997): *"I believe... I believe... I believe."*

Our Task

One mistake a person can make is to ignore the Blessed Virgin's injunctions. Another is to think that her call to conversion is meant for somebody else. "You speak much, little children, but you work little on your own conversion." (09/25/98)

"There are many who think they are doing a lot by talking about the messages but do not live them." (05/25/91) "Therefore, convert and start to live my messages, not with your words but with your life." (09/25/98)

"There are many who live in sin... Pray and fast for them." (03/21/84) "... I beseech all of you to pray, and help unbelievers by your prayers." (03/18/89)

"Pray in order to understand that all of you, through your life and your example, ought to collaborate in the work of salvation." (05/25/96) "God gave you the gift of holiness. Pray that you may understand it more and

7

more, and in that way you will be able to bear witness for
God by your life." (09/25/88)

Daily Meditation

"Therefore, little children, read every day the messages I have given you and incorporate them into your
life (12/25/89)," she beckons. We invite you to consider
adopting this book as part of your devotional reading,
perhaps focusing on one page a day. A way to benefit
greatly is to apply the teachings to your personal situation, pray for understanding, and put them into practice.

We offer the following as an example. Our Lady asks
us to pray "until prayer becomes joy for you."
(03/25/2000) Reflecting on this we may become aware
that we have been praying with a sense of futility and
hopelessness; there is hardly any joy. Then, in our peti-
tion for divine counsel we may be reminded of these
promises made by Jesus. "Ask, and it will be given to
you; search, and you will find; knock, and the door will
be opened to you. Everyone who asks receives; everyone
who searches finds; everyone who knocks will have the
door opened. Is there anyone among you who would
hand his son a stone when he asked for bread? Or would
hand him a snake when he asked for a fish? If you, then,
evil as you are, know how to give your children what is
good, how much more will your Father in heaven give
good things to those who ask him!" (Mt 7:7-11, New
Jerusalem Bible) "I tell you, therefore, everything you
ask and pray for, believe that you have it already, and it
will be yours." (Mk 11:24, New Jerusalem Bible) Con-
templating all of the above and taking them to heart, we

are blessed with the return of joy and peace in our prayers.

Do What Your Mother Says

In Jesus we see the perfect example of one who followed his Mother's bidding, with superlative fruitfulness. He lived in obedience to her for 30 years at Nazareth, and advanced in wisdom, in stature, and in favour before God and his people. (See Luke 2:51-52.)

"Dear children, if you live the messages, you are living the seeds of holiness." (10/10/85) Live the messages and you will know how true this statement is; you will receive help to be separated further from sin and profanity, you will become more and more united to God, you will understand your Christian vocation with greater clarity.

"Put God in the first place (01/25/2001)," the Blessed Virgin tells us. This is a key element and a link running through all of her instructions. It necessitates giving to God our highest regard, and trusting him explicitly. It requires our profound belief in his love, and learning to count on that love with complete abandonment and in the absence of the slightest trace of doubt. This is how we can "pray with the heart", full of confidence, joy and gratitude, reverently conscious of God's majestic presence in us and his tremendous affection for each one of us. He is ever mindful of the difficult situations we encounter; at the appropriate moment he will do all for our good.

Notes

1. Our Lady frequently addresses us as "Little children." In this, she echoes Jesus' words: "Unless you change and become like little children you will never enter the kingdom of Heaven." (Mt 18:3, New Jerusalem Bible) We are reminded over and over again to be childlike.

2. Mother Mary habitually closes her messages with, "Thank you for having responded to my call." This "Thank you" carries a special meaning. It has the same force as the ones seen in public places, like, "Thank you for not smoking", which signifies: "Do not smoke!" Besides expressing her gratitude, Our Lady is politely requesting, "Respond to my call! It is vital that you do."

3. For more information, please visit the above-mentioned Medjugorje parish sanctioned Internet site at *http://www.medjugorje.hr*. You might also wish to consult *WORDS FROM HEAVEN* by A Friend of Medjugorje (Saint James Publishing, Birmingham, Alabama, 2000). This work records Mary's sayings according to chronology, and offers three excellent indices for easy reference. We gratefully acknowledge the use of some excerpts and dates from it.

4. The quotations in *OUR LADY SPEAKS FROM MEDJUGORJE* are translated from the Croatian language. Should questions arise as to the interpretation of any text, they will have to be resolved by consulting the original document.

5. The subject titles are in alphabetical order, but, because the topics are not mutually exclusive, duplication and overlapping do exist here and there.

6. The numbers in brackets at the end of each citation denote the sequence (month/day/year). Thus, (08/15/86) indicates the communication was received on August 15, 1986.

TOPICS

ABANDON YOURSELVES TO GOD
AND TO MOTHER MARY

Whoever abandons himself to God does not have room in his heart for anguish. Difficulties will persist, but they will serve for spiritual growth and will render glory to God. (06/16/83)

Why do you not put your trust in me? I know that you have been praying for a long time; but you must really surrender yourself. Abandon your concerns to Jesus. Listen to what he says in the Gospel: "And who among you, through his anxiety, is able to add a single cubit to the length of his life? (Mt 6:27)" (10/30/83)

I have only one wish for tomorrow's feast [Immaculate Conception]. I ask of you to set aside at least a quarter of an hour to come before me and entrust your problems to me. No one on earth will understand you as I do. (12/07/85)

God will bestow great gifts on you if you surrender yourselves to him. (12/19/85)

Dear children, surrender to me so that I can lead you completely. (04/17/86)

God does not want you lukewarm or undecided, but that you totally surrender to him. (11/20/86)

Through prayer your Father will build you into the vessels he wants. For this, abandon yourselves completely to him. (07/11/87)

Put your life in God's hands. (01/25/88)

Therefore, dear children, forsake everything and consecrate your time to God and then God will bestow gifts upon you and bless you. Little children, do not forget that your life is transitory like the spring flower which today is wondrously beautiful, but tomorrow has vanished. Therefore, pray in such a way that your prayer, your surrender to God may become like a road sign. That way, your witness will not only have value for yourselves, but for all of eternity. (03/25/88)

I am calling you to total surrender to God. Pray, little children, that Satan does not sway you like branches in the wind. Be strong in God. I desire that through you the whole world may get to know the God of joy. Do not be anxious or worried. God will help you and show you the way. (05/25/88)

Everything you do and everything you possess give over to God so that he can take control in your life as King of all that you possess. (07/25/88)

Abandon yourselves to the Spirit for him to renew you. (05/05/89)

You see, little children, how nature is opening herself and is giving life and fruit. In the same way I am calling you to a life with God and complete surrender to him. (05/25/89)

ADORATION OF THE BLESSED SACRAMENT

Thank you for adoring my Son in the Sacred Host. That touches me very much. (01/26/84)

Unceasingly adore the Most Blessed Sacrament of the Altar. I am always present when the faithful are adoring. Special graces are then received by them. (03/15/84)

Your obligation is not so much to do, but to adore God, to stay with him. (06/24/86)

Today, I invite you to fall in love with the Most Holy Sacrament of the Altar. Adore him, little children, in your parishes; in this way you will be united with the entire world. Jesus will become your friend and you will

14

not talk of him as someone you hardly know. Union with him will be a joy for you, and you will become witnesses to the love of Jesus which he has for every creature. Little children, when you adore Jesus you are also close to me. (09/25/95)

APPARITIONS

I have come to call the world to conversion for the last time. Afterwards, I will not appear anymore on this earth. (05/02/82)

It is necessary to awaken the faith. It is a gift from God. If it were called for, I would appear in every home. (Spring/82)

These apparitions are the last in the world. (06/23/82)

BEAUTY

I am beautiful because I love. If you want to be beautiful, love. There is no one in the world who does not desire beauty. (03/25/85)

From day to day I wish to clothe you in holiness, goodness, obedience and God's love, so that from day to day you will become more beautiful and more prepared for your Master. (10/24/85)

How beautiful is the scenery when we look at nature in the morning in all its freshness! But how much more beautiful is it when we see a person bringing peace, love and happiness to others. (01/27/86)

Dear children, once again I want to call you to prayer. When you pray you are much more beautiful, like flowers which, after the snow, display all their beauty, and all their colours become indescribable. So also, dear children, after prayer you will show more strongly before

God everything that is beautiful; this pleases him. Therefore, dear children, pray, and open your inner self to the
Lord so that he may make of you a harmonious and
beautiful flower for Paradise. (12/18/86)

Put God at the centre of your being so that, in this
way, you can witness in joy the beauty that God continually gives in your life. (05/25/2001)

BIBLE

Dear children, today I call you to read the Bible every
day in your homes. And let it be in a visible place so as
to always encourage you to read it and to pray.
(10/18/84)

Every family must pray family-prayers and read the
Bible. (02/14/85)

Pray and read Sacred Scripture so that through my
coming here you may discover the message for you in
Sacred Scripture. (06/25/91)

Read Sacred Scripture, live it, and pray to understand
the signs of the time. This is a special time. That is why I
am with you to draw you close to my Heart and the Heart
of my Son Jesus. Dear little children, I want you to be
children of light and not of darkness. (08/25/93)

Little children, you do not know how to live in the
grace of God; that is why I call you anew to carry the
Word of God in your heart and in your thoughts. Little
children, place Sacred Scripture in a visible place in your
family, and read and live it. (08/25/96)

Little children, joyfully live the messages of the Gospel, which I am repeating in the time since I am with
you. Little children, I am your Mother and I desire to
reveal to you the God of love and the God of peace. I do

not desire for your life to be in sadness but that it be realized in joy for eternity according to the Gospel. Only in this way will your life have meaning. (12/25/96)

I call you to renew prayer in your families by reading Sacred Scripture and to experience joy in meeting with God who loves his creatures infinitely. (09/25/99)

CHANGE YOUR LIFE

It does not suffice to pray. You must change your life, your heart. (-/-/-)

I beg you, destroy the cardboard house which you have built on desires. In this way, I will be able to act for you. (-/-/86)

Dear children, I beseech you, begin to change through prayer and you will know what you need to do. (04/24/86)

Dear children, God blesses you day after day, and desires transformation of your life. Therefore, pray that you may have strength to change your life. (05/25/90)

I have come to help you, and therefore I invite you to change your life because you have taken a path of misery, a path of ruin. When I told you, "Convert, pray, fast, be reconciled", you took these messages superficially. You started to live them and then you stopped, because it was difficult for you. No, dear children, when something is good, you have to persevere in it, and not think, "God does not see me; he is not listening; he is not helping." (03/25/92)

I am close to you and intercede before God for each of you so that he may give you strength to change your heart. (01/25/98)

CHASTISEMENTS

I have prayed; the punishment [contained in the eighth secret] has been softened. Repeated prayers and fasting reduce punishments from God, but it is not possible to avoid the chastisement entirely. Go on the streets of the city, count those who glorify God and those who offend him. God can no longer put up with that. (11/06/82)

I will pray to my Son to spare you the punishment. Be converted without delay. You do not know God's plans; you will not be able to know them. You will not know what God will send, or what he will do. (04/25/83)

No pain, no suffering is too great for me in order to save you. I will pray to my Son not to punish the world; but I plead with you, be converted.

You cannot imagine what is going to happen or what the Eternal Father will send to earth. That is why you must be converted! Renounce everything. Do penance. Express my thanks to all my children who have prayed and fasted. I carry all this to my Divine Son in order to obtain the alleviation of his justice against the sins of mankind. (06/24/83)

I have always said that misfortune will only come if the world does not convert. Call the world to conversion. Everything depends on your conversion. (12/15/83)

In the world there are so many sins. What can I do if you do not help me. Remember that I love you. God does not have a hard heart. Look around you and see what people do, then you will no longer say that God has a hard heart. How many people come to church, the house of God, with respect and strong faith; how many love God? Very few! (10/25/85)

18

CHRISTMAS

Dear children, I am calling you to prepare yourselves for Christmas by means of penance, prayer, and works of charity. Dear children, do not look toward material things, because then you will not be able to experience Christmas. (12/05/85)

Dear children, for Christmas, my invitation is that together we glorify Jesus. I present him to you in a special way on that day, and my invitation to you is that on that day we glorify Jesus and his nativity. Dear children, on that day pray still more and think more about Jesus. (12/12/85)

Dear children, today I wish to call you to love of neighbour. The more you resolve to love your neighbour, the more you will experience Jesus especially on Christmas Day. God will bestow great gifts on you if you surrender yourselves to him. I wish in a special way on Christmas Day to give mothers my own special motherly blessing, and Jesus will bless the rest with his own blessing. (12/19/85)

Dear children, these are the days in which the Father grants special graces to all who open their hearts. I bless you and I desire that you too, dear children, become alive to the graces and place everything at God's disposal so that he may be glorified through you. (12/25/86)

You say that Christmas is a family feast day, therefore, dear children, put God in the first place in your families so that he may give you peace and protect you not only from war, but also from every Satanic attack during times of peace. When God is with you, you have everything. (12/25/91)

Today, again, I invite you to pray so that through prayer, fasting, and small sacrifices, you may prepare yourselves for the coming of Jesus. May this time, little children, be a time of grace for you. Use every moment and do good, for only in this way will you feel the birth of Jesus in your hearts. If you give good example with your life and become a sign of God's love, joy will prevail in the hearts of all. (11/25/96)

Today, on the birthday of my Son, my heart is filled with immeasurable joy, love, and peace. As your Mother, I desire for each of you to feel that same, joy, peace, and love in your heart. That is why, do not be afraid to open your heart and to completely surrender yourself to Jesus, because it is only in this way that he can enter into your heart and fill it with love, peace, and joy. (12/25/98)

I call you today and encourage you to prayer for peace. Especially today, carrying the new-born Jesus in my arms for you, I call you to unite with him through prayer and to become a sign to this peaceless world. Encourage each other, little children, to prayer and love. (12/25/2001)

CHURCH'S JUDGMENT ON MEDJUGORJE

One must follow the authority of the Church with certainty. Before She expresses an opinion, however, there must be spiritual progress, because She cannot pronounce judgment hastily. It takes place as with a birth that is followed by baptism and confirmation. The Church will confirm that which is born of God. We must walk and advance in the spiritual life, impelled by these messages. (-/-/86)

CONFESSION

Make your peace with God and among yourselves. For that, it is necessary to believe, to pray, to fast, and to go to Confession. (06/26/81)

One must invite people to go to Confession each month, especially on the first Saturday… Monthly Confession will be a remedy for the Church in the West. (08/06/82)

I am happy because you have begun to prepare for monthly observance of the Sacrament of Reconciliation. That will be good for the whole world. (10/01/82)

Do not go to Confession through habit, to remain the same after it. No, that is not good. Confession should give an impetus to your faith. It should stimulate you and bring you closer to Jesus. If Confession does not really mean something to you, it will be very difficult for you to be converted. (11/07/83)

May holy Confession be the first act of conversion for you and then, dear children, decide for holiness. (11/25/98)

CONSECRATION

I particularly protect those who have been consecrated to me. (08/31/82)

I wish that every Saturday, which is the day that the Church has dedicated to me, you will consecrate to me at least a quarter of an hour. Meditate during this time on my life, my messages; and pray. (05/28/83)

Consecrate yourself to my Immaculate Heart. There are some young people who have consecrated themselves to me, but there are some persons in the parish who are

21

not entirely consecrated... You have to consecrate yourself if you truly want to be better. (02/04/84)

Dear children, today I am very happy because there are many who want to consecrate themselves to me. Thank you. You have not made a mistake. My Son Jesus Christ wishes to bestow on you special graces through me. My Son is happy because of your dedication. (05/17/84)

Dear children, at this time it is especially necessary for you to consecrate yourselves to me and to my heart. (05/19/84)

Dear children, again today I call you to consecrate your life to me with love, so that I can guide you with love. (11/27/86)

Therefore, little children, I am calling you today to the prayer of Consecration to Jesus, my dear Son, so that each of your hearts may be his. And then I am calling you to Consecration to my Immaculate Heart. I want you to consecrate yourselves as individuals, families and parishes so that all belong to God through my hands. (10/25/88)

I call you to be responsible and determined, and to consecrate each day to God in prayer. (01/25/98)

CONSECRATION PRAYERS

CONSECRATION TO THE HEART OF JESUS
O Jesus, we know that you are merciful,
that you have given your Heart for us;
it was crowned with thorns by our sins.
We know that today you still pray for us
so that we will not be lost.

Jesus, remember us if we fall into sin.
Through your most Sacred Heart
make us all love one another.
Cause hatred to disappear among people.
Show us your love.
All of us love you
and desire that you protect us with your
Heart of the Good Shepherd.
Enter into each heart, Jesus!
Knock on the door of our hearts.
Be patient and persistent with us.
We are still locked up in ourselves
because we have not understood your will.
Knock continuously, O Jesus.
Make our hearts open up to you,
at least when we remember the Passion
which you suffered for us. Amen. (11/28/83)

CONSECRATION TO THE IMMACULATE HEART OF MARY

O Immaculate Heart of Mary, ardent with goodness,
show your love towards us.
May the flame of your Heart, O Mary,
descend on all mankind.
We love you so.
Impress true love in our hearts.
May our hearts yearn for you.
O Mary, sweet and humble of heart,
remember us when we are in sin.
You know that all of us are sinners.
By means of your Immaculate Heart, give us spiritual
health.

Let us always see the goodness of your maternal
   Heart,
and may we be converted by means of the flame of
   your Heart. Amen. (11/28/83)

CONVERSION
   Hurry to be converted. Do not wait for the great sign.
For the unbelievers, it will then be too late to be converted. For you who have faith, this time constitutes a
great opportunity for you to be converted and to deepen
your faith. (12/15/82)
   Help others to be converted, especially those who are
coming to Medjugorje. (01/30/86)
   Dear children, I want to lead you on the path of conversion and I wish that you convert the world, that your
life be conversion for others. (06/24/87)
   Today I invite you to conversion. This is the most important message that I have given you here. (02/25/96)
   Little children, when you put God in the first place,
then, in all that you do, you will seek the will of God. In
this way your daily conversion will become easier. Little
children, with humility seek out what is not in order in
your hearts. Conversion will become a daily duty that
you will perform with joy. Little children, I am with you,
I bless you all and I invite you to become my witnesses
by prayer and personal conversion. (04/25/96)
   Little children, you speak much about God, but you
witness little with your life. Therefore, little children,
decide for conversion, that your life may be true before
God, so that in the truth of your life you witness the
beauty God gave you. (07/25/96)

This, little children, is a time of grace for you. Make good use of it for your personal conversion, because when you have God, you have everything. (07/25/98)

You speak much, little children, but you work little on your own conversion. Therefore, convert and start to live my messages, not with your words but with your life. In this way, little children, you will have strength to decide for true conversion of the heart. (09/25/98)

Also today I call you to convert and to believe in God more firmly. (05/25/99)

You are concerned too much about material things and little about spiritual ones. Open your hearts and start again to work more on your personal conversion. (04/25/2000)

Little children, you live in a time in which God gives great graces but you do not know how to make good use of them. You are concerned about everything else, but least for the soul and the spiritual life. Awaken from the tired sleep of your soul and say "Yes" to God with all your strength. Decide for conversion and holiness. I am with you, little children, and I call you to perfection of your soul and of everything you do. (03/25/2001)

You cannot be converted, little children, if you do not abandon sins and do not decide for love towards God and neighbour. (01/25/2002)

CROSS, THE

Dear children, I want to tell you that the Cross should be central these days. Pray especially before the crucifix from which great graces are coming. Now in your homes make a special consecration to the crucifix. Promise that you will neither offend Jesus nor abuse the crucifix. (09/12/85)

Dear children, you will be able to receive Divine love only in the measure as you understand that on the Cross God offers you his immense love. (02/22/86)

Today, in a special way, I invite you to take the crucifix in your hands and meditate on the wounds of Jesus. Ask Jesus to heal your wounds which you, dear children, sustained during your life because of your sins or the sins of your parents. Only in this way, dear children, will you understand that the world is in need of healing and of faith in God the Creator. (03/25/97)

In this time of grace, may the Cross be a sign-post of love and unity for you through which true peace comes. (11/25/99)

DARKNESS

This unfaithful world is walking in darkness. (06/05/86)

Children, darkness reigns over the whole world. People are attracted by many things but they forget about what is more important. (07/30/87)

DECIDE FOR GOD

Dear children, I invite you to decide completely for God. (01/02/86)

I want you to realize that this life lasts briefly compared to the one in Heaven. Therefore, dear children, decide again for God. (11/27/86)

Dear children, when God calls people, it is really a great thing. Think how sad it would be to let those opportunities that God allows pass by without your taking them. So do not wait for tomorrow or the day after tomorrow. Say "Yes" to Jesus now! And may this "Yes" be for ever. (05/16/87)

The way is difficult for those who have not decided for God. Dear children, decide and believe that God is offering himself to you in his fullness. (10/25/87)

Today I invite you to decide for God once again, and to choose him before everything else and above everything else, so that he may work miracles in your life, and that day by day your life may become joy with him. (01/25/90)

I invite you to decide for God because distance from God is the fruit of lack of peace in your hearts. God is peace itself. Therefore, approach him through your personal prayer and then live peace in your hearts, and in this way peace will flow from your hearts like a river into the whole world. (02/25/91)

Decide to give more time to God who gave you these days of grace. Therefore, dear children, pray and renew in a special way the love for Jesus in your hearts. (03/25/91)

I invite you to decide for God; he will protect you and show you what you should do and which path you should take. (04/25/92)

At this time while you are still looking back to the past year I call you, little children, to look deeply into your heart and to decide to be closer to God and to prayer. Little children, you are still attached to earthly things and little to the spiritual life. May my call today be also an encouragement to you to decide for God and for daily conversion. (01/25/2002)

DO NOT LEAVE MOTHER MARY

Dear children! You have always prayed that I do not abandon you. Now I ask you in turn not to abandon me. Especially during these days, Satan wants to disperse you; because of that, pray very much at this time. Dear children, I came again to thank you. You have not yet understood what that means – to give joy to my heart. It is a very great thing. I ask you only to persevere in prayer. As long as you pray, I will have words for you. Good-bye. I thank you, dear children. My love for you is unlimited; be happy with me, because I am happy with you. (03/-/85)

DRAW NEAR TO GOD

I invite you to draw still closer to God through prayer. Only in this way will I be able to help and protect you from every attack of Satan. I am with you and I intercede for you with God, that he protect you. But I need your prayers and your "Yes". You get lost easily in material and human things and forget that God is your greatest friend. Therefore, my dear little children, draw close to God so that he may protect you and guard you from every evil. (02/25/92)

I am your Mother and I invite you to come closer to God through prayer, because he alone is your peace, your Saviour. Therefore, little children, do not seek comfort in material things. Rather, seek God. (09/25/93)

God gives himself to whoever seeks him. (04/25/97)

I am with you and I teach you, little children: in God is your peace and hope. Therefore, draw closer to God and put him in the first place in your life. (01/25/2001)

FAITH

There is only one God, one faith. Have the people believe firmly and not fear anything. (06/29/81)

Strengthen your faith through prayer and the sacraments. (08/08/81)

Prayer must become a part of your daily life to permit true faith to take root. (09/08/81)

Faith will not know how to be alive without prayer. (10/10/81)

The devil tries to impose his power on you, but you must remain strong and persevere in your faith. (11/-/81)

You who believe, be converted and deepen your faith. (Spring/83)

My children, do not believe everything that people tell you. One must not, because it weakens one's faith. (11/20/83)

If you would be strong in faith, Satan would not be able to do anything against you. (04/05/84)

Open your hearts and surrender your lives to Jesus so that he works through your hearts and strengthens you in faith. (05/23/85)

Therefore, little children, believe, and pray that the Father increase your faith, and then ask for whatever you need. (04/25/88)

I pray that you pray more strongly for peace and that you become more rooted in faith. (06/25/91)

I am near to you and I invite all of you, little children, into my embrace so that I may help you; but you do not want it, and so Satan puts you to the test, and in the smallest things your faith disappears. Therefore, little children, pray, and through prayer you will have blessing and peace. (03/25/95)

Listen, because I wish to speak to you and invite you to have more faith and trust in God who loves you immeasurably. (08/25/96)

May your faith be an encouragement to others to believe and to love more. (12/25/2001)

FALSE SEERS

That [prediction of disaster] comes from false prophets. They say, "On a certain day, at a certain date, there will be a catastrophe." I have always said that misfortune will only come if the world does not convert. Call the world to conversion. Everything depends on your conversion. (12/15/83)

Many pretend to see Jesus and the Mother of God and to understand their words, but they are, in fact, lying. It is a very grave sin, and it is necessary to pray very much for them. (-/-/84)

FAMILIES

May all families consecrate themselves to the Sacred Heart each day. I am very happy when the entire family meets to pray each morning for half an hour. (10/20/83)

Every family must pray family-prayer and read the Bible! (02/14/85)

Dear children, I beseech you to start changing your life in the family. Let the family be a harmonious flower which I desire to give to Jesus. Dear children, let every family be active in prayer for I wish that good fruit in the family be visible one day. Only in this way will I give all, like petals, as a gift to Jesus in fulfillment of God's plan. (05/01/86)

Therefore, dear children, let your family be a place where holiness is born. Help everyone to live in holiness, but especially your own family. (07/24/86)

The Holy Spirit wants to be present in families. Allow the Holy Spirit to enter. The Holy Spirit comes through prayer. That is why, pray and allow the Holy Spirit to renew you, to renew today's family. (07/03/89)

Dear children, tonight especially I would like to invite all parents in the world to find time for their children and family. May they give love to their children. (07/31/89)

In future I would like to see parents in families work and pray as much as they can with their children, so that from day to day they will be able to strengthen their spirit. (08/14/89)

Dear children, today I am inviting you to renewal of prayer in your families so that every family will become a joy to my Son Jesus. Therefore, dear children, pray and find more time for Jesus, and then you will be able to understand and accept everything, even the most difficult sicknesses and crosses. (01/25/92)

I want you to awaken love in your families so that love will reign where there is unrest and hatred. (04/25/93)

Satan wants to destroy the family. The family is in crisis. Pray. (06/25/95)

A family cannot say that it is at peace if it does not pray. Therefore, let your morning begin with morning-prayer, and the evening end with thanksgiving. Little children, I am with you and I love you. I bless you and I wish that every one of you be in my embrace. (08/25/95)

Teach your children, because if you are not an example to them, children depart into godlessness. (08/25/96)

Put Holy Scripture in a visible place in your families, read it, reflect on it and learn how God loves his people. (01/25/99)

Pray, dear children, particularly in this period, when Satan is trying to destroy your families. In a special way, dear children, pray with your children. May prayer live in your families. Be persistent. (09/20/99)

Renew prayer in your families and form prayer groups. (09/25/2000)

FASTING

The devil is trying to conquer you. Do not permit him. Keep faith; fast and pray. I will be with you at every step. (11/16/81)

If you do not have the strength to fast on bread and water, you can give up a number of things. It would be good to give up television, because after seeing some programs you are distracted and are unable to pray. You can give up alcohol, cigarettes, and other pleasures. You yourselves know what you have to do. (12/08/81)

The best fast is on bread and water. Through fasting and prayer one can stop wars, one can suspend the laws of nature. Works of charity cannot replace fasting. Those who are not able to fast can sometimes replace it with prayer, charity, and confession; but everyone, except the sick, has to fast. (07/21/82)

Repeated prayers and fasting reduce punishments from God. (11/06/82)

Besides Friday, fast an extra day a week on bread and water in honour of the Holy Spirit. (12/15/82)

If you pray and fast, you will obtain everything that you ask for. (10/29/83)

I want you to tell them that tomorrow is a day of fasting in order to sanctify yourselves in the Holy Spirit. (11/04/83)

I wish that prayer and fasting flourish in your hearts. (01/17/84)

I permit all those who wish to make a sacrifice to fast at most three times a week. May they not fast longer than that. (01/22/84)

May each one find his way to fast. He who smokes may abstain from smoking; he who drinks alcohol let him not drink. Let each one give up something which is dear to him. (03/01/84)

Pray and fast so that the kingdom of God may come among you. Let my Son set you aglow with his fire. (03/14/84)

Dear children, today I call on you to begin fasting with the heart. There are many people who are fasting, but only because everybody else is fasting. It has become a routine which no one is willing to discontinue. I ask the parish to fast out of gratitude because God has allowed me to stay so long in this parish. Dear children, fast and pray with the heart. (09/20/84)

Especially live the fast, because by fasting you will achieve - and cause me joy - the fulfilling of the whole plan, which God is planning here in Medjugorje. (09/26/85)

Pray. Fast. Let God act! (04/17/86)

I wish to renew prayer with you and to call you to fast. I desire to offer these to my Son Jesus for the coming of a new time – a time of spring. (10/25/2000)

Today I call you to renew prayer and fasting with even greater enthusiasm until prayer becomes a joy for you. (01/25/2001)

FATHER

Do not be afraid. Confide yourself to the Father. Pray until you are sure that he guides everything. (-/-/86)

O children! Remember: the only way for you to be always with me and to know the will of the Father is to pray… Continue to pray in spite of everything and you will understand the will of the Father and his love. (05/16/87)

Dear children! As a Mother, for many years already, I have been teaching you faith and love for God. Neither have you shown gratitude to the Father nor have you given him glory. You have become empty and your heart has become hard and without love for the sufferings of your neighbours. I am teaching you love and showing you that the Father has loved you, but you have not loved him. He sacrificed his Son for your salvation, my children. For as long as you do not love, you will not come to know the love of your Father. You will not come to know him because God is love. Love, and have no fear, my children, because in love there is no fear. If your hearts are open to the Father and if they are full of love towards him, then why fear what is to come? Those who do not love are afraid because they expect punishment and because they know how empty and hard they are. I am leading you, children, towards love, towards the Father. I am leading you into Eternal Life. (03/18/95)

FATIMA

I invite you to renunciation for nine days so that, with your help, everything I wanted to realize through the secrets I began in Fatima may be fulfilled. (08/25/91)

Therefore, dear children, help my Immaculate Heart to triumph in the sinful world. I beseech all of you to offer prayers and sacrifices for my intentions so that I can present them to God for what is most necessary. (09/25/91)

Pray for peace so that as soon as possible an era of peace, for which my heart waits impatiently, may reign. (06/25/95)

Dear children! I wish to share my joy with you. In my Immaculate Heart I feel that there are many who have drawn closer to me and, in a special way, carry the triumph of my Immaculate Heart in their hearts through prayer and personal conversion. I wish to thank you and inspire you to work even more for God and his kingdom with the love and power of the Holy Spirit. I am with you and I bless you with my motherly blessing. Thank you for having responded to my call. (08/25/2000)

FAULTS

I give you this advice: I would like you to try to conquer some fault each day. If your fault is to get angry at everything, try each day to get less angry. If your fault is inability to study, try to study. If your fault is not to be able to obey or put up with those who do not please you, try on a given day to speak with them. If your fault is that you cannot stand an arrogant person, you should try to approach this person. If you want that person to be humble, be humble yourselves. Show that humility is worth more than pride. Thus, each day, try to go a little further and cast off every vice from your heart. Find out which vices you need to eliminate most. (02/20/85)

You will be happy if you do not judge yourselves according to your faults, but if you understand that even in your faults graces are offered to you. (05/12/86)

FEAR NOT!

Be persevering and courageous. Do not fear anything. (02/25/82)

In Holy Scripture you have heard it said, "Do not worry about tomorrow, each day will have its own troubles." [See Mt 6:34] Then do not worry about other days. Be content with prayer. I, your Mother, will take care of the rest. (02/29/84)

You must forget what is behind you in your life. I only want you to become a new person from now on. Do not fear anything when I am near you. I love you. (-/-/-)

Dear children, sometimes you burden your hearts with certain things, and this is not necessary. Sometimes you are afraid of this or that. Why do you need to do this? Whoever is with Jesus need not fear. Do not be anxious about what will happen tomorrow or a few years from now. Surrender yourselves to Jesus; only in this way will you be sheep that follow their shepherd. (-/-/-)

Do not be afraid of Satan. That is not worth the trouble, because with a humble prayer and an ardent love, one can disarm him. (08/-/85)

You do not have to be afraid because you know that Jesus will never leave you, and you know that he leads you to salvation. (08/11/86)

Little children, the one who prays is not afraid of the future, and the one who fasts is not afraid of evil. Once

36

again, I repeat to you: it is only through prayer and fasting that even wars can be stopped – the wars of your unbelief and fear for the future. (01/25/2001)

And you, do not be afraid because the one who prays is not afraid of evil and has no hatred in his heart. (09/25/2001)

FORGIVENESS

I am a Mother, and even though I feel pain for each one who goes astray, I forgive easily, and am happy for every child who returns to me. (11/14/85)

The fruit of peace is love and the fruit of love is forgiveness. I am with you and I invite all of you, little children, to forgive in the family first of all, and then you will be able to forgive others. (01/25/96)

Dear children, pray with the heart to know how to forgive and to be forgiven. (06/25/97)

FUTURE

The only attitude of the Christian toward the future is hope of salvation. Those who think only of wars, evils and punishment do not do well. If you think of evil, punishment and wars, you are on the road to meeting them. Your responsibility is to accept Divine peace, to live it, and to spread it. (08/-/84)

Today I call you to prayer. The one who prays is not afraid of the future. Little children, do not forget, I am with you and I love you all. (06/25/2000)

GIFT

Always accept immediately the gifts which I give you so that you can profit from them. (06/11/84)

Each of you has a special gift which is personal. You alone can understand it interiorly. (07/-/85)

If you have received a gift from God you must be appreciative, but do not say that it is yours. Say, rather, that it is God's. (09/10/85)

Dear children, my heart is full of grace and love. My heart is the gift I give you. (06/16/87)

Little children, understand also the greatness of the gift which God is giving you through me. (03/25/90)

Do not forget that your life does not belong to you, but is a gift with which you must bring joy to others and lead them to Eternal Life. (12/25/92)

In the goodness and love of God the Creator, I am also with you as a gift. (10/25/95)

GLORIFY GOD

God will give you gifts with which you will glorify him till the end of your life on this earth. (06/02/84)

Therefore, little children, renew prayer in your families and your heart will glorify the holy name of God, and heaven will reign in your hearts. (05/25/97)

Also today, I call you to give glory to God the Creator in the colours of nature. He speaks to you also through the smallest flower about his beauty and the depth of love with which he has created you. Little children, may prayer flow from your hearts like fresh water from a spring. May the wheat fields speak to you about the mercy of God towards every creature. (08/25/99)

GOD

Take me seriously. When God comes among people he does not come to joke but to say serious things. (-/-/83)

When God begins his work, no one can stop it. (04/04/83)

God offers himself to you. (11/25/88)

God wants to save all of you. (03/25/90)

God is your greatest friend. (02/25/92)

Little children, when God is in the first place, then you will, in all that you do, seek the will of God. (04/25/96)

May each day be a joyful witness for you of God's love. (06/25/99)

In a special way, now when it is being said that God is far away, he has truly never been nearer to you. (09/25/99)

I call you to prayer so that through prayer you put God in the first place. (11/25/2000)

Put God at the centre of your being so that, in this way, you can witness in joy the beauty that God continually gives in your life. (05/25/2001)

GOODNESS

These are the days when you need to decide for God, for peace, and for good. May all hatred and jealousy disappear from your life and from your thoughts, and may only love for God and neighbour dwell there. Thus and only thus will you be able to discern the signs of this time. (01/25/93)

Also today I rejoice with you and I call you to goodness. I desire that each of you reflect and carry peace in your heart, and say, "I want to put God first in my life." In this way, little children, each of you will become holy. Little children, tell everyone, "I want goodness for you," and he will respond with goodness, and, little children, good will come to dwell in the heart of each person. (12/25/97)

GRACE

The world is on the point of receiving great favours from me and my Son. (11/15/81)

All graces are at your disposal. All you have to do is take them. In order to do that, I tell you, pray! (09/12/83)

God allows me to help you every day with graces to defend yourselves against evil. This is my month. I want to give it to you. Just pray and God will give you the graces you are seeking. (10/25/84)

You do not understand the messages which God is sending you through me. He is giving you great graces but you do not know it. Pray to the Holy Spirit for enlightenment. If you only knew how great are the graces that God is granting you, you would pray without ceasing. (11/08/84)

Dear children, during these days my Lord is allowing me to intercede for more graces for you. Therefore, I wish to urge you once more to pray, dear children! Pray without ceasing! (06/19/86)

Dear children, seek from God the graces which he is giving you through me. I am ready to intercede with God for all that you seek so that your holiness may be complete. Therefore, dear children, do not forget to seek, because God has permitted me to obtain graces for you. (08/25/87)

GROWTH

I want great peace and love to grow in you. Consequently, pray! (09/29/83)

Strive to make your joy grow, to live in faith, to change your hearts. (12/07/83)

I want to call you to grow in love. A flower cannot grow without water. So you also, dear children, cannot grow without God's blessing. You need to seek his blessing from day to day so that you will grow normally and perform all your actions in union with God. (04/10/86)

I desire that through each one of you God's plan may be fulfilled, and that everything God has planted in your heart may keep on growing. (04/25/87)

Build yourself up spiritually. This building-up lasts until the end of your life. (03/27/89)

HEALING

Have strong faith, pray and fast, and they [the sick] will be healed. Be confident and rest in joy. Go in the peace of God. (11/26/81)

Pray for the sick. Believe firmly. I will come to help according to what is in my power. I will ask my Son Jesus to help them. In the meantime, the most important thing is a strong faith. (02/09/82)

For the healing of the sick, it is important to say the following prayers: the Creed, and seven times each the Lord's Prayer, the Hail Mary, and the Glory Be, and to fast on bread and water. It is good to lay one's hands on the sick and to pray. It is good to anoint the sick with holy oil. Not all priests have the gift of healing. In order to receive this gift, the priest must pray with perseverance and believe firmly. (07/25/82)

Let them believe and pray; I cannot help those who do not pray and offer sacrifices. The sick, just like those who are in good health, must pray and fast for the sick. The firmer you believe, the more you pray and fast for the same intention, the greater is the grace and the mercy of God. (08/18/82)

I cannot cure. God alone cures. Pray! I will pray with you. Believe firmly. Fast, do penance. I will help you as long as it is in my power to do so. God comes to help everyone. I am not God. (-/-/83)

Pray! What is most important for your body is prayer. (12/22/83)

Many have begun to pray for healing here at Medjugorje, but when they return to their homes they abandon prayer, forget, and then lose many graces. (09/12/86)

HEART

Place an image of the hearts of Jesus and Mary in your homes. (11/11/83)

Do not think that Jesus will manifest himself again in the manger; friends, he is born again in your hearts. (01/08/84)

I desire to live in your hearts. (02/05/84)

Open your hearts to me, I desire to bless them fully. (02/11/84)

Give me your hearts. I desire to change them completely. I desire them to be pure. (02/13/84)

I expect generosity and prayer from your hearts. (02/21/84)

I desire to stay in your hearts always and for you to stay in mine. (02/24/84)

I wish that your hearts would be united to mine, just as my heart is united to that of my Son. (03/28/84)

Dear children, this evening I pray that you venerate especially the Heart of my Son Jesus. Make reparation for the wounds inflicted on the Heart of my Son. That Heart is offended by all kinds of sins. (04/05/84)

Dear children, today I thank you for every opening of your hearts. Joy overtakes me for every heart that is opened to God especially from the parish. Rejoice with me! Pray all the prayers for the opening of sinful hearts. I desire that. God desires that through me. (04/18/85)

Work and change your hearts so that a new spirit from God can take its place in your hearts. (04/25/85)

Turn your hearts toward prayer and seek the Holy Spirit to be poured out on you. (05/09/85)

Open your hearts and surrender your life to Jesus so that he may work through your hearts. (05/23/85)

A heart which belongs to the Lord is splendorous, even if it is flooded with difficulties and trials. But if the heart engaged in difficulties strays away from God, it loses its splendour. (06/25/85)

A person's heart is like a brilliant pearl. When it belongs completely to the Lord, it shines even in the darkness. But when it is divided, a little for Satan, a little for sin, a little for everything, it fades and is no longer worth anything. (06/-/85)

Everything has its own time. Today I call you to start working on your hearts. Now that all the toil in the fields is over, you are finding time for cleaning even the most neglected areas, but you leave your heart aside. Work more and, with love, clean every part of your heart. (10/17/85)

You are wondering, dear children, why you cannot respond to what I seek from you. You are unable because you have not given me your hearts so that I can change them. (05/15/86)

Dear children, today I call you prepare your hearts for these days when the Lord particularly desires to purify you from all the sins of your past. You, dear children, are not able by yourselves; therefore I am here to help you. You pray, dear children! Only in that way will you be able to recognize all the evil that is in you and surrender it to the Lord so that the Lord may completely purify your hearts. Therefore, dear children, pray without ceasing and prepare your hearts in penance and fasting. (12/04/86)

Satan is strong and therefore, dear children, by constant prayer press tightly to my motherly heart. (10/25/88)

I am with you and I keep watch unceasingly over every heart which is given to me. (02/25/89)

I invite you, little children, to help me through your prayers so that as many hearts as possible come close to my Immaculate Heart. (05/25/95)

Consecrate your heart and make it the home of the Lord. May he dwell in it forever. (03/18/96)

Little children, with humility seek out what is not in order in your hearts. (04/25/96)

Your hearts, little children, are still not completely open to me, and therefore I invite you again to open yourselves to prayer so that in prayer the Holy Spirit will help you: that your hearts become of flesh and not of stone. (06/25/96)

Reflect and pray, and then God will be born in your heart, and your heart will be joyous. (08/25/96)

I am with you and I intercede before God for each of you so that your heart receives the gift of conversion. Only in this way, little children, will you understand the importance of grace in these times and God will become nearer to you. (04/25/98)

Dear children, today I call you to come closer to my Immaculate Heart. (10/25/98)

Children, you seek peace and pray in different ways, but you have not yet given your hearts to God for him to fill them with his love. So, I am with you to teach you and to bring you closer to the love of God. If you love God above all else, it will be easy for you to pray and to open your hearts to him. (05/25/99)

Dear children! Do not seek peace and happiness in vain, in the wrong places and in the wrong things. Do not permit your hearts to become hard by loving vanity. (03/18/2000)

I carry all of you in my heart, and I bless you with my motherly blessing. (09/25/2000)

Come closer to my heart so that I can lead you to my Son Jesus. (06/25/2001)

Open yourselves to prayer and seek from God the conversion of your hearts; everything else he sees and provides. (04/25/2002)

HEAVEN

The person who has done much evil during his life can still go straight to Heaven if he confesses, is sorry for what he has done, and receives Communion at the end of his life. (07/24/82)

Do not attribute importance to petty things. Long for Heaven. (07/25/87)

Today I want to call all of you to decide for Paradise. (10/25/87)

In Heaven you will receive the Father's reward which he has promised you. (02/25/88)

I am here, dear children, to help you and to lead you to Heaven. (05/25/91)

Little children, I am your Mother, I love you, and I want each of you to be saved and thus be with me in Heaven. (08/25/98)

Do not forget that you are here on earth on the way to eternity and that your home is in Heaven. Therefore, little children, be open to God's love and leave egoism and sin. (07/25/2000)

HELL

I have shown you Hell so that you may know the state of those who are there. (11/06/81)

Today many persons go to Hell. God allows his children to suffer in Hell due to the fact that they have committed grave, unpardonable sins. Those who are in Hell no longer have a chance to know a better lot. (07/25/82)

People who go to Hell no longer want to receive any benefit from God. They do not repent nor do they cease to revolt and blaspheme. They make up their minds to live in Hell and do not contemplate leaving it. (01/10/83)

HOLINESS

Today I am calling you to holiness. Without holiness you cannot live. (07/10/86)

Dear children, I rejoice because of all of you who are on the way of holiness. And I beseech you, by your personal witness, to help those who do not know how to live holiness. Therefore, dear children, let your family be a place where holiness is born. Help everyone to live in holiness, but especially your own family. (07/24/86)

You know that I want to lead you on the way of holiness, but I do not want to compel you by force to be saints. I wish that each one of you will help yourself and me by your own little self-denials so that I can lead you to holiness day by day. (10/09/86)

Especially, dear children, I call you to begin to live in holiness by your prayers and sacrifices. For I want each of you who has been to this fountain of grace to come to Paradise with the special gift which you will give me, that is, holiness. Therefore, dear children, pray, and daily change your life in order to become holy. (11/13/86)

I love you and therefore I want you to be holy. I do not want Satan to block you on that way. Dear children, pray and accept all that God is offering you on a way which is bitter. But at the same time, God will reveal every sweetness to whoever begins to go on that way, and who gladly answers every call of God. (07/25/87)

Dear children, God wants to make you holy. Therefore, through me he is calling you to complete surrender. (04/25/88)

God gave you the gift of holiness. Pray that you may understand it more and more, and in that way you will be able to bear witness for God by your life. (09/25/88)

May your conversion and decision for holiness begin today and not tomorrow. (11/25/98)

Today I call all of you to decide for holiness. May holiness be for you, little children, always in the first place in your thoughts and in each situation, in work and in speech. In this way you will also put it into practice; little by little, step by step, prayer and the decision for holiness will enter into your family. (08/25/2001)

HOLY OBJECTS

Place an image of the hearts of Jesus and Mary in your homes. (11/11/83)

I call you to place more blessed objects in your homes, and I call everyone to put some blessed object on yourself. Let all the objects be blessed, and thus Satan will attack you less because you will have armour against him. (07/18/85)

Carry blessed objects with you. Put them in your house, and restore the use of holy water. (11/-/91)

HOLY SPIRIT

Begin each day by calling on the Holy Spirit. The most important thing is to pray to the Holy Spirit. When the Holy Spirit descends on earth then everything becomes clear, and everything is transformed. (-/-/83)

Let yourself be guided in depth by the Holy Spirit, then your work will go well. Do not hurry. Let yourself be guided and you will see that everything will be accomplished well. (07/04/83)

The important thing is to pray to the Holy Spirit so that he may descend on you. When one has him, one has everything. (10/21/83)

I have asked you to pray always and at all times that the Holy Spirit descend upon all of you. (01/02/84)

Ask the Holy Spirit to renew your souls, to renew the entire world. (03/05/84)

Pray to the Holy Spirit so that he may enlighten you, and you will come to know all that you wish. (05/26/84)

Dear children, tonight I want to tell you during the days of this novena to pray for the outpouring of the Holy Spirit on your families and on your parish. Pray, and you will not regret it. (06/02/84)

The most important thing in the spiritual life is to ask for the gift of the Holy Spirit. When the Holy Spirit comes, peace will be established. When that occurs, everything changes around you. (10/-/84)

The Holy Spirit wants to be present in families. Allow the Holy Spirit to enter. The Holy Spirit comes through prayer. That is why, pray and allow the Holy Spirit to renew you, to renew today's family. (07/03/89)

Dear children, this is a time of grace. Open yourselves to the Holy Spirit, for the Holy Spirit to make you strong. (06/01/90)

I invite you to open yourselves to God by means of prayer so that the Holy Spirit may begin to work miracles in you and through you... Therefore, dear little children, pray, pray, pray, and do what the Holy Spirit inspires you to do. (05/25/93)

The Holy Spirit will enlighten you to understand that you must convert. (07/25/95)

Dear children, today I call you to prepare yourselves, through prayer and sacrifice, for the coming of the Holy Spirit… May your heart be prepared to listen to, and live, everything that the Holy Spirit has in his plan for each of you. Little children, allow the Holy Spirit to lead you on the way of truth and salvation towards eternal life. (05/25/98)

Pray, little children, that the Holy Spirit may come to dwell in you in fullness so that you may be able to witness in joy to all those who are far from faith. Especially, little children, pray for the gifts of the Holy Spirit so that in the spirit of love, every day and in each situation, you may be closer to your fellowmen, and that you may overcome every difficulty in wisdom and love. (05/25/2000)

Bless and seek the wisdom of the Holy Spirit to lead you at this time so that you may comprehend and live in the grace of this time. (05/25/2001)

HUMILITY

I desire humility from you, but you can become humble only through prayer and fasting. (02/10/84)

Pray for the peace and humility of your hearts. (02/12/84)

Carry my messages with humility in such a way that, on seeing happiness in you, people will want to be like you. Do not carry my messages just to throw them at others. (07/-/85)

Today I invite you to live in humility all the messages which I am giving you. In living the messages do not become arrogant and say, "I am living the messages." If you carry and live the messages in your heart, everyone will feel it, so that there will be no need for words which serve those who do not obey. (09/20/85)

All that you do for others do with great joy and humility towards God. (11/25/90)

INTERMEDIARY

There is only one mediator between God and man, and that is Jesus Christ. (10/07/81)

I do not dispose all graces. I receive from God what I obtain through prayer. (08/31/82)

Jesus prefers that you address yourselves directly to him rather than through an intermediary. In the meantime, if you wish to give yourselves completely to God and if you wish that I be your protector, then confide to me all your intentions, your fasts, and your sacrifices so that I can dispose of them according to the will of God. (09/04/82)

I beseech you, pray to Jesus. I am his Mother, and I intercede for you with him. But all prayers go to Jesus. I will help, I will pray, but everything does not depend solely on me, but also on your strength, and the strength of those who pray. (-/-/83)

JESUS

I am your Mother full of goodness, and Jesus is your great friend. Do not fear anything in his presence. Give him your heart. From the bottom of your heart tell him your sufferings; you will then be invigorated in prayer, your heart will be free and in peace without fear. (11/29/83)

You know well that when a friend asks you for something, you give it to him. It is thus with Jesus. When you pray without ceasing, and you come in spite of your tiredness, he will give you all that you ask from him. (12/01/83)

How can you not be happy? Jesus gives himself to you. (04/14/84)

Raise your hands, yearn for Jesus because in his Resurrection he wants to fill you with graces. (04/21/84)

Open your hearts and surrender your life to Jesus so that he may work through your hearts. (05/23/85)

Dear children, open your hearts and let Jesus guide you. For many people it seems to be hard, but it is so easy! (08/11/86)

Dear children, give all problems and difficulties to Jesus, and pray. (02/29/88)

Pray and renew in a special way the love for Jesus in your hearts. (03/25/91)

Let little Jesus reign in your hearts and only then, when Jesus is your friend, will you be happy. It will not be difficult for you either to pray or to offer sacrifices, or to witness Jesus' greatness in your life, because he will give you strength and joy in this time. (11/25/93)

I desire, little children, to guide you all to Jesus because he is your salvation. (06/25/94)

By your daily life, little children, you will become an example and witness whether you live for Jesus or against him and his will. (03/25/98)

Dear children, thank my Son for all the graces that he has given you. (06/25/99)

Invoke the name of my Son. Receive him in your heart. Only in the name of my Son will you experience true happiness and true peace in your heart. Only in this way will you come to know the love of God and to spread it further. (03/18/2000)

In this time of grace, I call you to become friends of Jesus. (02/25/2002)

Today I call you to unite with Jesus in prayer. Open your heart to him and give him everything that is in it: joys, sorrows and illnesses. May this be a time of grace for you. Pray, little children, and may every moment belong to Jesus. (03/25/2002)

JOY

Let joy reign in your hearts. (04/20/84)

I wish only that you would be happy, that you be filled with joy, that you be filled with peace and proclaim this joy. (-/-/86)

I am joyful, but my joy is not complete until you are filled with joy. You are not yet filled with joy because you are not yet at the stage of understanding my immense love. (10/-/86)

I want each one of you to be happy; but in sin nobody can be happy. Therefore, dear children, pray, and in prayer you will realize a new way of joy. Joy will manifest itself in your hearts and thus you will be joyful witnesses of what my Son and I want from each one of you. (02/25/87)

I desire that through you the whole world may get to know the God of joy. (05/25/88)

Today I invite you all to rejoice in the life which God gives you. Little children, rejoice in God the Creator because he has created you so wonderfully. Pray that your life will be a joyful thanksgiving which flows out of your hearts like a river of joy. Little children, give thanks unceasingly for all that you possess, for each little gift which God has given you, so that a joyful blessing always comes down from God upon your life. (08/25/88)

My dear children, these are days of joy. Give me all your problems, and live in joy. (12/24/88)

I would like each one of you to discover the joy and the love that exist only in God and that only God can give. (05/25/89)

Decide everyday to dedicate time to God and to prayer until prayer becomes a joyful meeting with God for you. Only in this way will your life have meaning and with joy you will contemplate eternal life. (04/25/2000)

I desire to share my joy with you. (08/25/2000)

Little children, you are chosen to witness peace and joy. (10/25/2001)

LENT

During this Lent, you should try and truly desire to spend it in love. Strive as much as possible. (02/20/85)

This Lent is a special incentive for you to change. Start from this moment. Turn off the television and renounce various things that are of no value. Dear children, I am calling you individually to conversion. This season is for you. (02/13/86)

The second message of these Lenten days is that you renew prayer before the crucifix. Dear children, from the crucifix I give you special graces and Jesus gives you special gifts. Take them and live! Reflect on Jesus' Passion, and be united with Jesus in your life! (02/20/86)

Today I call you to live this Lent by means of little sacrifices. Thank you for every sacrifice you have made. Dear children, live that way continuously, and with your love help me to present the sacrifice. God will reward you for that. (03/13/86)

Thank you for the things you have renounced during Lent. Most of all, renounce sin. Be light to shine for others. Encourage others to prayer, fasting and penance. Give love to others. (02/22/88)

Dear children, in this period of Lent, Satan tries by every means to destroy in you what we have started. I caution you as a Mother, let prayer be your weapon against him. (03/14/88)

Dear children, remember the four things you have to do during Lent. Tonight when you go home, I ask you to be thankful in front of the crucifix for all that you feel you should be grateful for; thank Jesus for what you want. My Son will hear you. (02/13/89)

I ask you again to multiply your prayers to prepare yourself for Easter. Also, read the Bible, especially those passages that speak about the Passion of Jesus. Prepare yourself to look at Jesus eye to eye. Tonight when you come home, pray in front of the crucifix in thanksgiving for all the graces you have received. (03/17/89)

LIGHT

In your life you have all experienced light and darkness. God grants to every person that he recognizes good and evil. I am calling you to light which you should carry to all the people who are in darkness. People who are in darkness come into your homes daily. Dear children, give them light! (03/14/85)

Especially, dear children, I wish that all of you be the reflection of Jesus, which will enlighten this unfaithful world walking in darkness. I wish all of you to be light for everyone and that you give witness in the light. Dear children, you are not called to darkness, but you are called to the light. Therefore, live the light with your life. (06/05/86)

Light will not reign in the world until people accept Jesus, until they live his words, which is the Word of the Gospel. (07/30/87)

Dear children, be a light that shines. (08/12/88)

Through you, I wish to renew the world. Understand, little children, that today you are the salt of the earth and the light of the world. (10/25/96)

Be light, and illuminate all souls where darkness reigns. (03/02/97)

Cast all darkness out of your heart and allow God's light and God's love to enter into your heart and to dwell there forever. Be carriers of God's light and love to all mankind, so that all may feel and experience in you and through you the true light and love which only God can give. (12/25/99)

Peacelessness has begun to reign in hearts and hatred reigns in the world. That is why, you who live the messages be the light and extended hands to this faithless world that all may come to know the God of Love. (11/25/2001)

LOVE

Love your neighbour. May harmony reign among you. (12/24/81)

Love one another, my children. You are brothers and sisters. Do not argue among yourselves. (12/25/81)

Be calmer, more poised. Do not take sides with other children. Be agreeable, well-mannered, pious. (02/12/82)

Love your enemies. Banish from your heart hatred, bitterness, and preconceived judgments. Pray for your enemies and call the divine blessing upon them. (06/16/83)

I wish to engrave in every heart the sign of love. If you love all mankind, there will be peace in you. If you are at peace with all men, it is the kingdom of love. (01/18/84)

Love everyone on earth, just as you love yourselves. (02/28/84)

Love is a gift from God. Therefore, pray that God may give you the gift to love. (05/28/84)

Dear children, you need love. (06/08/84)

Dear children, through love you will achieve everything, even that which you think is impossible. (02/28/85)

You should do everything out of love. Accept with love all annoyances, all difficulties, everything. Dedicate yourselves to love. (03/09/85)

I am beautiful because I love. If you want to be beautiful, love. (03/25/85)

Always have the love of God in you, because without this love you cannot convert completely. (06/01/85)

I am calling you to love of neighbour and love toward the one from whom evil comes to you. In that way you will be able to discern the motives of the heart. (11/07/85)

Pray, so that the Kingdom of Love may come into the whole world. How happy mankind would be if love reigned! (03/25/86)

Dear children, today my call to you is that in your life you live love towards God and neighbour. Without love, dear children, you can do nothing. Therefore, dear children, I am calling you to live in mutual love... Start loving from today with an ardent love, the love with which I love you. (05/29/86)

If you do not love, you will not be able to transmit the testimony; you will not be able to witness either for me or for Jesus. (06/06/86)

Therefore, obtain victory against every sin through love. With love, overcome all the difficulties that come to you. (07/10/86)

Hatred gives birth to dissension and does not have respect for anyone or anything. I call you to always bring harmony and peace. Especially, dear children, in the place where you live, act with love. Let your sole instrument always be love. By love turn everything into good... (07/31/86)

If you want to love, pray for your brothers and sisters. (-/-/-)

You know that I love you and that I am burning with love for you. Therefore, dear children, decide also for love so that you will long for and experience the love of God daily. Dear children, decide for love so that love prevails in all of you, but not human love, rather, God's love. (11/20/86)

If you love from the bottom of your heart, you receive a lot. If you hate, you lose a lot. Dear children, love makes great things. The more you have love inside you, the more you can love people around you. That is why, pray unceasingly to Jesus for him to fill your hearts with love. (04/12/87)

O children, I want you to live each new day with love and peace. I want you to be the carriers of peace and love. (07/11/87)

Love your Serbian, Orthodox and Muslim brothers, and the atheists who persecute you. Most of all I want you to offer prayers for my children who do not know my love and the love of my Son. Help them to come to know it! (-/-/87)

Pray, because in prayer each one of you will be able to achieve complete love. (10/25/87)

I want you to love all people with my love, both the good and the bad. Only in that way will love conquer the world. (05/25/88)

Today I am calling you to the love which is loyal and pleasing to God. Little children, love bears everything bitter and difficult for the sake of Jesus who is love. Therefore, dear children, pray that God will come to your aid, not, however, according to your desires but according to his love. Surrender yourselves to God so that he may heal you, console you, and forgive everything inside you which is a hindrance on the way of love. In this way, God can mold your life and you will grow in love. (06/25/88)

I would like to give you love, so that you can bring this love and spread it to others. (10/17/88)

I wish that your whole life be love, only love. Everything that you do, do with love. In every little thing, see Jesus and his example. Do as Jesus did. He died out of love for you, so you must also offer all you do to God with love, even the smallest little things of everyday life. (11/30/88)

Dear children, I want you to witness my presence through love. (11/26/90)

I want to draw you ever closer to Jesus and to his wounded heart so that you may be able to comprehend the immeasurable love which was given to each one of you. Therefore, dear children, pray that a fountain of love will flow from your heart to every person, including the one who hates you and the one who despises you. That way, through Jesus' love, you will be able to overcome all the misery in this sorrowful world which is without hope for those who do not know Jesus. (11/25/91)

I call you to first love God, the Creator of your lives; then you will be able to recognize and love God in every person as he loves you. (11/25/92)

Love, and have no fear, my children, because in love there is no fear. (03/18/95)

If you do not first love God, then you will neither be able to love neighbour nor the one you hate. (04/25/95)

Without love, little children, you cannot grow in holiness, and you cannot do good deeds. (11/25/95)

Dear children, pray for your brothers who have not experienced the love of the Father, for those whose only importance is life on earth. Open your hearts towards them and see in them my Son who loves them. (03/02/97)

As Mother, I ask that you do not go on the path that you have been on, that is, the path without love towards neighbour and towards my Son. On this path, you will find only hardness and emptiness of heart, and not peace for which all of you long. (03/18/97)

Dear children, today I call you to understand that without love you cannot comprehend that God has to be in the first place in your life. That is why, little children, I call you all to love, not with a human love, but with God's love. In this way, your life will be more beautiful and without self-interest. You will comprehend that, out of love, God gives himself to you in the simplest way. Little children, so that you may comprehend my words which I give out of love, pray, pray, pray, and you will be able to accept others with love and to forgive all who have done evil to you. (09/25/97)

Little children, I desire that you become apostles of love. By your love, little children, you will be recognized as mine. (03/25/98)

Little children, today I am near you and I bless each of you with my Motherly blessing so that you may have strength, and love for all the people you meet in your earthly life, and that you can give them God's love. (11/25/2000)

Do not forget that I am with you, and I desire to take all of you to my Son that he may give you the gift of sincere love towards God and towards everything that is from him. (04/25/2002)

MASS

Listen attentively at Mass. Be well-mannered. Do not chat during Mass. (02/19/82)

The Mass is the greatest prayer of God. You will never be able to understand its greatness. That is why you must be perfect and humble at Mass, and you should prepare yourselves for it. (-/-/83)

You must behave well; be pious and set a good example for the faithful. (04/21/83)

Before Mass it is necessary to pray to the Holy Spirit. (11/-/83)

Be kind enough to come to Mass without looking for an excuse. Show me that you have a generous heart. (12/02/83)

My children, I wish that the Mass be for you the gift of the day. Attend it, wish for it to begin. Jesus gives himself to you during Mass. (03/30/84)

When you go to Mass, your trip from home to church should be a time of preparation for it. You should also receive Holy Communion with an open and pure heart... Do not leave the church without an appropriate act of thanksgiving. (10/-/84)

You are not celebrating Holy Mass as you ought to. If you knew what graces and gifts you would receive you would prepare yourselves at least an hour for each Mass. (-/-/85)

I wish your Mass to be an experience of God. (05/16/85)

Dear children, strive to go deep into the Mass as you should. (06/01/85)

Come to Mass because this is the season given to you. Dear children, there are enough who come regularly despite bad weather; they come because they love me and want to show their love in a special way. What I want from you is to show me your love by coming to Mass, and the Lord will reward you abundantly. (11/21/85)

There are many of you who have sensed the beauty of the Mass, but there are also those who come unwillingly. I have chosen you, dear children, but it is Jesus who gives you his graces at Mass. Therefore, live Holy Mass consciously, and let your coming to it be joyful. Come to it with love, and make the Mass your own. (04/03/86)

Let Holy Mass be your life. (04/25/88)

Pray all three mysteries of the Rosary daily for non-believers, and attend Mass especially for them once a month. (03/08/91)

May Holy Mass, little children, not be a routine for you, but life. By living Holy Mass each day, you will feel the need for holiness and you will grow in holiness. (01/25/98)

MATERIALISM

Do not concern yourself too much with the things of this world, but entrust all in prayer to our Heavenly Father. If a person is very preoccupied, he will not be able to pray well because internal serenity is lacking. God will do his part in bringing about a successful conclusion to the things of here below if one strives to work for the things of God. (06/16/83)

You are absorbed with material things, but in material things you lose everything that God wishes to give you. I call you, dear children, to pray for the gifts of the Holy Spirit which are necessary in order to enable you to give witness now to my presence here and to all that I am giving you. Dear children, surrender to me so that I can lead you completely. Do not be absorbed with material things. (04/17/86)

Pray, because you are in the midst of great temptation and danger, for the world and material goods lead you into slavery. Satan is active in this plan. (06/25/89)

You get lost easily in material and human things and forget that God is your greatest friend. Therefore, my dear little children, draw close to God so that he may protect you and guard you from every evil. (02/25/92)

Therefore, little children, do not seek comfort in material things. Rather, seek God. (09/25/93)

In this time, due to the spirit of consumerism, when one forgets what it means to love and to cherish true values, I invite you again, little children, to put God first in your life. Do not let Satan attract you through material things but, little children, decide for God who is freedom and love. (03/25/96)

I invite you to reflect on your future. You are creating a new world without God, but only with your own strength. That is why you are dissatisfied and without joy in the heart. This time is my time, and therefore, little children, I invite you again to pray. When you find union with God, you will feel hunger for the kingdom of God, and your heart, little children, will overflow with joy. (01/25/97)

Be real with yourselves and do not bind yourselves to material things but to God. And do not forget, little children, that your life is transitory like a flower. (08/25/2001)

MEDJUGORJE PARISH

Dear children, I have chosen this parish in a special way and I wish to lead it. I am guarding it in love, and I want everyone to be mine. (03/01/84)

Dear children, you in the parish, be converted... That way all those who will come here will be able to convert. (03/08/84)

Today I beseech you to stop slandering and to pray for the unity of the parish, because my Son and I have a special plan for this parish. (04/12/84)

Dear children, tomorrow night pray for the Spirit of Truth, especially you from the parish. Because you need the Spirit of Truth to be able to convey the messages just the way they are, neither adding anything to them, nor taking anything whatsoever away from them, but just the way I said them. Pray for the Holy Spirit to inspire you with the spirit of prayer, so that you will pray more. I, your Mother, tell you that you are not praying much. (06/09/84)

I pray for the priests and the parishioners, that no one may be troubled. I know the changes which will take place soon. At the time of the changes, I will be there. Also, do not be afraid; there will be signs in the future concerning sinners, unbelievers, alcoholics, and young people. They will accept me again. (07/16/84)

Dear children, I beseech you, especially those from this parish, to live my messages and convey them to others, to whomever you meet. (08/16/84)

Dear children, today I want to thank you for all your sacrifices, but I give special thanks to those who have become dear to my heart and come here gladly. There are enough parishioners who are not listening to the messages, but, because of those who are close to my heart in a special way, because of them, I am giving messages for the parish. And I will go on giving them because I love you and I want you to spread my messages with your heart. (01/10/85)

These days Satan is manifesting himself in a special way in this parish. Pray, dear children, that God's plan is brought into effect and that every work of Satan ends up for the glory of God. (02/07/85)

From day to day I have been inviting you to renewal and prayer in the parish, but you do not accept. Today I am calling you for the last time! Now it is Lent, and you as a parish can turn to my messages out of love during Lent. If you do not do that, I do not want to give messages to you. (02/21/85)

God wants this parish to belong completely to him. And that is what I want too. (02/28/85)

Dear children, I love you. I have chosen this parish in a special way, because it is dearer to me than all others. I have gladly remained here when the Almighty sent me. Therefore, I call on you: accept me, dear children, that it may go well with you. Listen to my messages. (03/21/85)

Today is the day when I had wished to stop giving the messages because some individuals did not accept me. The parish has responded well and therefore I wish to give you messages as it has never been done in history from the beginning of the world. (04/04/85)

You, members of this parish, have a large and heavy cross to bear; but do not be afraid to carry it. My son is here to help you. (04/05/85)

Today I wish to tell everyone in the parish to pray in a special way to the Holy Spirit for enlightenment. From this day forward, God wants to test the parish in a special way in order that he might strengthen it in faith. (04/11/85)

During these days people from all nations will be coming into the parish. And now I am calling you to love: love first of all your own household members, and then you will be able to accept and love all who are coming here. (06/06/85)

These days you have felt great joy because of all the people who have come and to whom you could tell your experiences with love. Now I invite you to continue in humility and with an open heart, speak to all those who come here. (06/28/85)

I love this parish, and with my mantle I protect it from every work of Satan. Pray that Satan retreats from the parish and from every individual who comes into the parish. In that way you will be able to hear every call of God and answer it with your life. (07/11/85)

Today I wish to tell you that I have chosen this parish and that I am guarding it in my hands like a little flower that does not want to die. I call you to surrender to me so that I can continue presenting you to God, fresh and without sin. (08/01/85)

This parish, which I have chosen, is special and different from others. I am giving great graces to all who pray with the heart. Dear children, I am giving messages first of all to the residents of the parish, and then to all the others. First you must accept the messages, then others will accept them too. (02/06/86)

You are the ones responsible for the messages. The source of grace is here, but you, dear children, are the vessels which transport the gifts. Therefore, dear children, I am calling you to do your job with responsibility. Each one will be responsible according to his ability. Dear children, I am calling you to give the gifts to others with love, and not to keep them for yourselves. (05/08/86)

Without love, dear children, you can do nothing. Therefore, dear children, I am calling you to live in mutual love. Only in that way will you be able to love and accept both me and all those around you who are coming into your parish. Everyone will sense my love through you. (05/29/86)

Dear children, today I invite you in a special way to pray for the plans of God to be fulfilled: first of all with you, then with this parish which God himself has chosen. Dear children, to be chosen by God is truly something great, but it is also a responsibility for you to pray more, for you, the chosen ones, to encourage others so you can be a light for people in darkness. (07/30/87)

The people here will be witnesses of the love of God. (06/25/88)

I want you to understand that I desire to realize here not only a place of prayer but also a meeting of hearts. I desire that my heart, and Jesus', and yours, become one heart of love and peace. That is why, little children, pray and rejoice over everything that God does here, in spite of Satan provoking quarrels and unrest. I am with you and I lead you all on the way of love. (07/25/99)

MESSAGES

It is necessary to tell them [some questioning priests] that, from the very beginning, the message I have been conveying to the world is of God. It is a great pity not to believe in it. Faith is a vital element, but one cannot compel a person to believe. (12/31/81)

You are not fully appreciative of the messages which God is sending you through me. He is giving you great graces and you do not comprehend them. Pray to the Holy Spirit for enlightenment. (11/08/84)

Dear children, I desire to keep on giving you still further messages, not every Thursday however, but on the 25th of each month. The time has come when what my Lord wanted has been fulfilled. Now I will give you fewer messages but I am still with you. Therefore, dear children, I beseech you, listen to my messages and live them, so that I can guide you. (01/08/87)

For years I have been inviting you by the messages which I am giving you. Little children, by means of the messages I wish to make a very beautiful mosaic in your heart so that I may be able to present each one of you to God like the original image. (11/25/89)

Therefore, little children, accept with seriousness and live the messages so that your soul may not be sad when I will not be with you anymore and when I will not guide you anymore like an insecure child in his first steps. Therefore, little children, read every day the messages I have given you and incorporate them into your life. I love you and therefore I call all of you to the way of salvation with God. (12/25/89)

God gives me this time as a gift to you, so that I may instruct and lead you on the path of salvation. Dear children, now you do not comprehend this grace, but a time will come soon when you will lament for these messages. (08/25/97)

MESSAGES, LIVE THEM

Today I call you to listen to my messages and then you will be able to live everything that God tells me to convey to you. (07/25/85)

Dear children, if you live the messages, you are living the seeds of holiness. (10/10/85)

Dear children, listen to and live my messages. I wish to guide you. (10/24/85)

My dear children! I come to you in order to lead you to purity of soul and then to God. How have you listened to me? At the beginning you carried on without believing but with fear and defiance toward these young people whom I have chosen; then afterwards, most of you listened to me in your hearts and began to carry out my maternal requests. But that did not last long. Whenever I come to you my Son comes with me, but so does Satan. Without noticing it, you permitted his influences on you, and he drives you away. Sometimes you understood that something you did was not agreeable to God, but soon you no longer paid attention to it.

Do not let that happen, my children. Wipe from my face the tears I cry in seeing what you do. Wake up. Take time to meet with God in the church. Come to visit in your Father's house. Take time to meet among yourselves for family-prayer, and implore the grace of God. Remember your deceased. Give them joy by the celebration of Holy Mass. Do not look with scorn on those who beg you for a piece of bread. Do not turn them away from your full tables. Help them and God will also help you. Perhaps it is in this way that God will hear you, and the blessing that he wants to give you in gratitude will be realized.

You have forgotten all this my children. Satan has influenced you also in this. Do not let that happen! Pray with me! Do not deceive yourselves into thinking, "I am good, but my brother next door is not good." You would be wrong. I, your Mother, love you, and it is for that reason that I am cautioning you about this.

Concerning the secrets, my children, these are not known by the people. But when they will learn of them, it will be too late. Return to prayer! There is nothing more important! I would dearly wish that the Lord would permit me to enlighten you a little more on these secrets, but the grace which is offered to you is already great enough.

Think how much you have offended him. What are you offering him of yourself? When was the last time you renounced something for the Lord? I no longer wish to reprimand you in this way, but I want to invite you once more to prayer, fasting and penance. If you wish to obtain a grace from God by fasting, let no one know that you are fasting. If you wish to receive a grace from God by a gift to the poor, let no one know that you have given this gift. Listen to me, my children! Meditate on my message in prayer. (01/28/87)

I do not want you, dear children, to live the message and be committing sin; that displeases me. (03/25/87)

I ask you to renew in yourselves the messages I have given you. These are messages of prayer, peace, fasting, and penance. Do some penance yourselves. All of the other messages come from these four basic ones. (06/06/88)

Dear children, I seek your action, not your words! You are all happy when I give you a beautiful message; but live all the messages I give! May each message lead you to new growth. Take this message into your life; in this way you will grow in life. Your Mother cannot give you other messages if you do not live the ones I have already given you. Begin tonight to live the messages. (02/17/89)

I invite all of you who have heard my message of peace to realize it in your life with seriousness and love. There are many who think that they are doing a lot by talking about the messages but do not live them. (05/25/91)

Pray, dear children, and have more trust in me, because I am here in order to help you, and to guide you on a new path towards a new life. Therefore, dear little children, listen and live what I tell you because it is important for you to remember my words and all that I have told you when I will no longer be with you. (10/25/92)

Dear children, the fact of my being with you is a grace! Therefore, accept and live my messages for your own good. (11/25/92)

I invite you all to have more trust in me and to live my messages more deeply. I am with you and I intercede before God for you, but I also wait for your hearts to open up to my messages. (05/25/94)

Dear children! Also today I am with you and call all of you to renew yourselves by living my messages. (10/25/97)

By fasting and prayer witness that you are mine and that you live my messages. (04/25/99)

MESSAGES, SPREAD THEM

Preach my messages. Speak about the events at Medjugorje. (09/29/83)

I am anxious for people to know what is happening in Medjugorje. Speak about it so that all will be converted. (1984/1985)

I wish you to be active in living and spreading the messages. (06/05/86)

Dear children, today I invite you to become missionaries of my messages which I am giving here through this place that is dear to me. God has allowed me to stay this long with you, and therefore, little children, I invite you to live with love the messages I give and to transmit them to the whole world, so that a river of love flows to people who are full of hatred and without peace. (02/25/95)

Little children, I wish that each of you become a carrier of my messages. (02/25/96)

MONEY

Each Thursday, read again the passage of Matthew 6:24-34 before the Most Blessed Sacrament. If it is not possible to come to the church do it at home with your family. (03/01/84)

Read each Thursday the Gospel of Matthew where it is said: "No one can serve two masters.... You cannot serve God and money." [Matthew 6:24] (08/05/86)

MOTHER MARY HELPS YOU

God allows me every day to help you with graces to defend yourselves against evil. (10/25/84)

I am your Mother and I desire to help you. (06/19/86)

I am with you and I desire to help you with my prayers and I desire to guide you on the path of peace. (10/25/90)

God sends me to help you and to guide you towards Paradise, which is your goal. (09/25/94)

I do not want your hearts to wander in today's darkness. I will help you. (03/18/99)

MOTHER MARY IS WITH YOU

The wind is my sign. I will come in the wind. When the wind blows, know that I am with you. (02/15/84)

I want to be with you always. I want to stay in your hearts always, and for you to stay in mine. (02/24/84)

Little children, do not be afraid because I am with you even when you think there is no way out and that Satan is in control. I am bringing peace to you. (07/25/88)

Little children, I am with you and unceasingly I want to lead you to the joy of life. (05/25/89)

I am with you and wish to lead you on the path to salvation which Jesus gives. From day to day I am closer and closer to you, although you are not conscious of it and do not want to admit that you are only slightly connected to me in prayer. (05/25/92)

I am with you, and everyday I bless you with my Motherly Blessing, so that the Lord may fill you with the abundance of his grace for your daily life. Thank God for the gift of my being with you, because I am telling you: this is a great grace. (07/25/92)

Dear children, I am with you and I rejoice today because the Most High has granted me to be with you and to teach you, and to guide you on the path of perfection. (10/25/94)

I am with you. I carry all of you in my heart. (09/25/2000)

Do not forget, little children, I am with you and bless you all. (11/25/2001)

MOTHER MARY LOVES YOU

I, the Mother, love you all. At any moment that is difficult for you, do not be afraid! Because I love you even when you are far from my Son and me. (05/24/84)

If you knew how much I love you, you would cry with joy. (06/21/84)

My love for you is unlimited; be happy with me, because I am happy with you. (03/-/85)

You do not know, dear children, how great my love is, and you do not know how to accept it. In various ways I wish to show it to you, but you, dear children, do not recognize it. You do not understand my words with your heart, and neither can you understand my love. (05/22/86)

You know, dear children, that I love you immeasurably, and I pray daily that the Lord will help you comprehend the love which I am showing you. (08/21/86)

I love you, dear children, with a special love, and I desire to bring all of you to Heaven unto God. I want you to realize that this life lasts briefly compared to the one in Heaven. Therefore, dear children, decide again for God. Only in that way will I be able to show how very dear you are to me and how much I desire all to be saved and to be with me Heaven. (11/27/86)

I love you, dear children, and so, not even counting the number of times, I go on calling you. (06/25/87)

I am your Mother, I love you all equally, and I intercede for you before God. (02/25/94)

Little children, you are dear to me. I love you all, and I call you to be closer to me and that your love towards my Immaculate Heart be more fervent. (10/25/96)

Little children, do not forget, I am with you and I love you all. (06/25/2000)

MOTHER MARY NEEDS YOU AND YOUR CO-OPERATION

I invite you. I need you. I chose you. You are important. (06/-/81)

Dear children, without you I am not able to help the world. I desire that you co-operate with me in everything, even in the smallest things. Therefore, dear children, help me by letting your prayer be from the heart, and by all of you surrendering completely to me. (08/28/86)

You know, dear children, that with your help I can accomplish everything and force Satan not to seduce you to evil and to remove himself from this place. (09/04/86)

Dear children, I would like this time to be the time of decision. Make a decision, dear children, follow me, follow me! I cannot do anything, and I want to do a lot, but I cannot do it without you. (08/19/88)

I want to collaborate with you, for I need your collaboration. Dear children, I want you to become my announcers and my children who will bring peace, love and conversion... I want you to be a sign for others. (01/02/89)

Dear children, tonight I wish to call you again to prayer because I need your help for the fulfillment of my plans. I need your participation, dear children. (02/12/90)

Today is the day of Peace, but throughout the whole world there is much lack of peace. Therefore, I call you to build up a new world of peace together with me, by means of prayer. Without you, I cannot do that, and therefore, I call all of you with my Motherly love, and God will do the rest. (12/25/92)

Never as much as today is my heart begging for your help! I, your Mother, am begging my children that they help me fulfill what the Father has sent me to do. (01/02/2000)

MOTHER MARY NEEDS YOUR PRAYERS

Tell the faithful that I need their prayers, and prayers from all the people. It is necessary to pray as much as possible and do penance because very few people have been converted up until now. There are many Christians who live like pagans. There are always so few true believers. (-/-/84)

How many persons have followed other beliefs or sects and have abandoned Jesus Christ! They create their own gods; they adore idols. How that hurts me! If only they could be converted! How large in number are the unbelievers! That will change only if you help me with your prayers. (02/09/84)

I ask you to pray for the conversion of everyone. For that, I need your prayers. (04/08/84)

I still need your prayers. You wonder why all these prayers? Look around you, dear children, and you will see how greatly sin has dominated the world. Pray, therefore, that Jesus conquers. (09/13/84)

Your prayers are necessary to me so that God may be glorified through all of you. (01/16/86)

Children, here is the reason why I need your prayer: prayer is the only way to save the human race. (07/30/87)

Dear children, I need your prayer to fulfill the plans I have with you now and also in the world. (03/23/90)

Most of all I wish that you dedicate prayers for my children who do not know my love and the love of my Son. Help them to come to know it! Help me as the Mother of all of you! (03/18/91)

Your prayers are necessary to me; through them I desire to bring you closer to God. (09/25/94)

MOTHER MARY PRAYS FOR YOU

I will intercede for you to God for all your intentions. (11/24/88)

I promise you, my children, that I will pray for you. (03/18/91)

I pray for you and intercede before God for peace: first for peace in your hearts, then around you, so that God may be your peace. (06/25/92)

I am praying and interceding for you before God that you convert, that your life and conduct be always Christian. (04/25/99)

I am with you and I intercede for each of you before Jesus. (05/25/2000)

MOTHER MARY PROTECTS YOU

Pray, pray. In this way I will protect you. (12/12/83)

I want to protect you under my mantle. (11/27/88)

Dear children, I am with you even if you are not conscious of it. I want to protect you from everything that Satan offers you and through which he wants to destroy you. (03/25/90)

Dear children, these times are special, and therefore I am with you to love and protect you, to protect your hearts from Satan and to bring you all closer to the heart of my Son Jesus. (06/25/93)

MOTHER MARY THANKS YOU

Thank the people in my name for the prayers, the sacrifices, and the penance. Have them persevere in prayer, fasting, and conversion, and have them wait with patience for the realization of my promise. Everything is unfolding according to God's plan. (06/25/82)

Today I thank you for all the prayers. Continue praying all the more so that Satan will be far away from this place. Dear children, Satan's plan has failed. Pray for the fulfillment of what God plans in this parish. I especially thank the young people for the sacrifices they have offered up. (09/05/85)

I thank you for the love which you are showing me. (08/21/86)

Dear children, I desire to thank you for every response to the messages. Especially, dear children, thank you for all the sacrifices and prayers which you have presented to me. (01/08/87)

I thank you for all that you are doing for my intentions. (06/25/87)

Thank you, dear children, for listening to me. (03/23/90)

I thank you because your response is serving God and peace. (01/25/91)

Dear children, tonight your Mother wants to say, "Thank you." Thank you for all your prayers, you who have prayed and helped me up to this day so that I am realizing my plans. (08/19/94)

Little children, thank you for having responded to my call and for having decided to walk with me toward holiness. (06/25/96)

Today I thank you for living and witnessing my messages with your life. (06/25/99)

NEW TIME

I am with you, and I guide you into a new time, a time which God gives you as grace so that you may get to know him more. (01/25/93)

I am with you and I present you to Jesus in a special way, now in this new time in which one should decide for him. (12/25/95)

I wish to renew prayer with you and to call you to fast. I desire to offer these to my Son Jesus for the coming of a new time – a time of spring. (10/25/2000)

Rejoice with me in this time of spring when all nature is awakening and your hearts long for change. Open yourselves, little children, and pray. (04/25/2002)

OASIS OF PEACE

God permits me to bring about this oasis of peace together with him. I wish to call on you to protect it and that the oasis be always unspoiled. There are those who are destroying peace and prayer by their carelessness. I invite you to give witness and to help to preserve peace by your life. (06/26/86)

You know that I promised you an oasis of peace, but you do not know that beside an oasis stands the desert where Satan is lurking and wants to tempt each one of you. Dear children, it is only by prayer that you can overcome every influence of Satan in your place. (08/07/86)

OPENNESS TO GOD AND TO MOTHER MARY

Dear children, today I wish to tell you to open your hearts to God like the spring flowers which crave for the sun. I am your Mother and I always want you to be closer to the Father, and that he will always give abundant gifts to your hearts. (01/31/85)

These days I call you especially to open your hearts to the Holy Spirit. Especially during these days the Holy Spirit is working through you.

Open your hearts and surrender your lives to Jesus so that he may work through your hearts and strengthen you in faith. (05/23/85)

Open yourselves to God and God will work through you and keep on giving you everything you need. (07/25/85)

Open yourselves to God and surrender all your difficulties and crosses to him so that he may turn everything into joy. Little children, you cannot open yourselves to God if you do not pray; therefore, from today, decide to consecrate a time and a day solely for meeting with God in silence. (07/25/89)

Your Mother is here to help each one of you. Open your hearts to your Mother; she is waiting for you. (08/14/89)

Open yourselves to the Holy Spirit, for the Holy Spirit to make you strong. (06/01/90)

I am telling you again to open your hearts to me and allow me to lead you. My way leads to God. (03/18/94)

I invite you to open yourselves to me and become an instrument in my hands for the salvation of the world. Little children, I want all of you who have felt the fragrance of holiness through these messages which I am giving you, to carry this fragrance into the world which is hungry for God and for his love. (03/25/94)

Dear children, today I invite you to open yourselves to God the Creator, so that he changes you. (10/25/96)

Open your heart and give time to God so that he will be your friend. When true friendship with God is realized no storm can destroy it. (06/25/97)

Today, I call you to open yourselves completely to me so that I may transform you and lead you to the heart of my Son Jesus, so that he can fill you with his love. Only in this way, little children, will you find true peace – the peace that only God gives you. (10/25/98)

Little children, open your hearts and give me everything that is in them: joys, sorrows and every pain, even the smallest one, that I may offer them to Jesus, so that with his immeasurable love he may burn and transform your sorrows into the joy of his resurrection. That is why, I now call you in a special way, little children, for your hearts to open to prayer, so that through prayer you may become friends of Jesus. (02/25/99)

In this Jubilee year many hearts have opened to me, and the Church is being renewed in the Spirit. I rejoice with you and I thank God for this gift. (10/25/2000)

PEACE

Peace. Peace. Peace. Be reconciled. Only peace. Make your peace with God and among yourselves. For that, it is necessary to believe, to pray, to fast, and to go to Confession. (06/26/81)

Dear children, without prayer there is no peace. Therefore, I say to you, dear children, pray at the foot of the cross for peace. (09/06/84)

You will not have peace through presidents, but through prayer. (12/31/85)

Dear children, by your own peace I am calling you to help others to see and begin to seek peace. (09/25/86)

May this time be the time in which all of us give and distribute peace to others. Therefore, please spread peace in your homes, in your families, in the streets, and everywhere. (03/21/88)

Dear children, I would like to tell you to bring peace to others during these days. Encourage others to change. Dear children, you cannot give peace if you yourselves do not have inner peace. (08/12/88)

Live peace in your heart and in your surroundings, so that all may recognize the peace which does not come from you but from God. (12/25/88)

Today I call you to pray in a special way and to offer up sacrifices and good deeds for peace in the world. Satan is strong and, with all his strength, tries to destroy the peace which comes from God. (10/25/90)

Therefore, pray that the Lord of Peace may protect you with his mantle and that he may help you to comprehend the greatness and the importance of peace in your hearts. In this way, you will be able to spread peace from your hearts throughout the whole world. I am with you and I intercede for you before God. Pray, because Satan wants to destroy my plans of peace. Be reconciled with one another, and by means of your lives help that peace may reign upon the whole earth. (12/25/90)

God is peace itself. Therefore, approach him through your personal prayer and then live peace in your hearts, and in this way peace will flow from your hearts like a river into the whole world. Do not speak about peace, but make peace. (02/25/91)

You are the ones who will bring peace to the world. (06/24/92)

Today I rejoice with you, and I pray with you for peace; peace in your hearts, peace in your families, peace in your desires, and peace in the whole world. May the King of Peace bless you today and give you peace. (12/25/94)

I invite you to open the door of your heart to Jesus as the flower opens itself to the sun. Jesus desires to fill your hearts with peace and joy. Little children, you cannot realize peace if you are not at peace with Jesus. Therefore, I invite you to Confession so that Jesus may be your truth and peace. (01/25/95)

I pray for you, and I intercede for you before God so that you may comprehend that each of you is a carrier of peace. You cannot have peace if your heart is not at peace with God. That is why, little children, pray, pray, pray, because prayer is the foundation of your peace. (06/25/97)

Yearn for peace and seek it. (12/25/98)

This is a time of grace. Little children, today in a special way with little Jesus whom I hold in my embrace, I am giving you the possibility of deciding for peace. Through your 'Yes' for peace and your decision for God, a new possibility for peace is opened to you. Only in this way, little children, will this century be for you a time of peace and well-being. (12/25/99)

I call you today to give peace to others. Only in God is there true peace. Open your hearts and become people who give the gift of peace. Others will discover peace in you and through you, and in this way you will be a witness of the peace and love which God gives you. (01/25/2000)

Witness peace to every heart and be carriers of peace in this peace-less world. (09/25/2001)

Little children, you are chosen to witness peace and joy. If there is no peace, pray and you will receive it. Through you and your prayer, little children, peace will begin to flow through the world. That is why, little children, pray, pray, pray, because prayer works miracles in human hearts and in the world. (10/25/2001)

PENANCE

You cannot imagine what is going to happen or what the Eternal Father will send to earth. That is why you must be converted! Renounce everything. Do penance. Express my thanks to all my children who have prayed and fasted. I carry all this to my Divine Son in order to obtain the alleviation of his justice against the sins of mankind. (06/24/83)

It is necessary to pray as much as possible and do penance because very few people have been converted up until now. There are many Christians who live like pagans. There are always so few true believers. (-/-/84)

PERSEVERENCE

Be persevering! Pray! Many people are beginning to convert. (11/01/81)

Be patient. Everything is developing according to God's plan. His promises will be realized. Continue to pray, to do penance, and to be converted. (04/21/82)

Continue your efforts and be persevering and tenacious. Pray without ceasing. (12/08/83)

In a special way this evening, I am calling you to perseverance in trials. (03/09/84)

In this time, Satan wants to create disorder in your hearts and in your families. Little children, do not give in. You must not permit him to lead you and your life. I love you and intercede for you before God. Little children, pray! (01/25/94)

PLAN

Everything is unfolding according to God's plan. (06/25/82)

Rejoice with me and with my angels, because a part of my plan has already been realized. Many have been converted, although many still do not want to be converted. (03/25/84)

Keep on praying that my plans be completely achieved. (09/27/84)

Pray with me so that God's plan may be realized through your prayers and mine. Pray more, and more intensely. (10/24/84)

My dear children, Satan is strong. He wishes with all his strength to destroy my plans. Just pray, and do not stop doing it. I will also pray to my Son so that all the plans that I have begun will be fulfilled. (01/14/85)

And offer your sacrifices to Jesus in order that everything may be fulfilled the way he has planned it, and that Satan will accomplish nothing. (01/09/86)

Dear children, today I call you all to pray that God's plans for you, and everything that God desires through you, may be realized! (01/30/86)

Dear children, I want you to understand that God has chosen each one of you so as to use you in a great plan for the salvation of mankind. You cannot comprehend how great your role is in God's design. Therefore, dear children, pray, so that in prayer you may know the plan of God for you. I am with you in order that you may bring it about in all its fullness. (01/25/87)

POPE JOHN PAUL II

He is your father, the spiritual father of all. It is necessary to pray for him. (11/08/81)

His enemies have wanted to kill him, but I protected him. (05/13/82)

God has given him permission to defeat Satan. (09/16/82)

Have him consider himself the father of all mankind and not only of Christians. Have him spread untiringly and with courage the message of peace and love among all humankind. (09/26/82)

In my messages, I recommend to everyone, and to the Holy Father in particular, to spread the message which I received from my Son here at Medjugorje. I wish to entrust to the Pope the word with which I came here, '**PEACE**', which he must spread everywhere. Here is a message which is especially for him: that he bring together the Christian people through his word and his preaching, that he spread, particularly among the young people, the messages which he has received from the Father in his prayer during which time God inspires him. (09/16/83)

You must warn the Bishop very soon, and the Pope, with respect to the urgency and great importance of the message for all mankind. I have already said many times that the peace of the world is in a state of crisis. (11/30/83)

I ask you to pray in a special way for Pope John Paul II and for priests. (07/10/92)

Pray, little children, for the health of my most beloved son [John Paul II], who suffers and whom I have chosen for these times. (08/25/94)

PRAY FOR OUR LADY'S INTENTIONS

In these days, I ask you to pray for my intentions. (07/01/83)

I know that you prayed today and that you did all your work while praying. Still, I have a particular intention for which I ask you to say each day the Lord's Prayer seven times, seven Hail Mary's, and the Creed. (10/31/83)

If you pray for my intentions, I will be glorified through you. All your prayers are going to help you through my hands. (11/26/88)

Dear children, I love you, and I want you to pray for my intentions with the love you have for me, so that every plan of God concerning each one of you may be fulfilled. (12/15/88)

I invite you to decide to pray for my intentions. Dear children, offer novenas, making sacrifices wherein you feel the most bound. I want your life to be tied to me. (07/25/93)

Today I wish to open my motherly heart to you and to call you all to pray for my intentions. I wish to renew prayer with you and to call you to fast. I desire to offer these to my Son Jesus for the coming of a new time – a time of spring. (10/25/2000)

PRAYER

I ask you to pray only with fervour. Prayer must become a part of your daily life to permit true faith to take root. (09/08/81)

I have made promises to you; it is up to you to pray and to persevere. Also, be without anxiety.

Faith will not survive without prayer. (10/10/81)

Continue to pray, because prayer is the salvation of the people. (12/09/81)

Pray and believe firmly. Say the prayers which have already been requested – the Lord's Prayer, the Hail Mary, and the Glory Be seven times each, and the Creed. (04/24/82)

Through fasting and prayer, one can stop wars, one can suspend the laws of nature. (07/21/82)

The most beautiful prayer is the Creed. (-/-/83)

All prayers are good, if they are said with faith. (-/-/83)

Those who attend school or go to work must pray half an hour in the morning and in the evening, and if possible, participate at Mass. It is necessary to extend the spirit of prayer to daily work, that is to say, to accompany work with prayer. (06/16/83)

Be careful not to diminish the spirit of prayer. (08/15/83)

When I give you this message, do not be content to just listen to it. Increase your prayer and see how it makes you happy. All graces are at your disposal. All you have to do is take them. In order to do that, I tell you, pray! (09/12/83)

Dear children, one lives not only from work. One lives also from prayer. (Autumn/83)

If you pray, a source of life will flow from your hearts. (10/24/83)

Prayer is the only road which leads to peace. If you pray and fast, you will obtain everything that you ask for. (10/29/83)

Pray also in the evening when you have finished your day. Sit down in your room and say to Jesus, "Thank you." In the evening, if you fall asleep in peace and in prayer, then in the morning you will wake up thinking of Jesus. You will then be able to pray for peace. But if you fall asleep in distraction, the day after will be misty, and you will even forget to pray that day. (10/30/83)

You can do everything; yes, you can do it through prayer. (11/11/83)

Pray, and do it with fervour. Include the whole world in your prayer. (11/13/83)

Pray, because prayer is life. (11/14/83)

If I am always asking you to pray, do not think that your prayers are not good. But I invite you to prolong your personal prayer, and to pray more intensely for others. (11/17/83)

My children, pray and keep your soul pure. (11/27/83)

Prayer should not be just a habit for you, but a source of happiness. You should live by prayer. (12/04/83)

I wish that prayer be renewed in your heart every day. Pray more, yes, more each day. (12/11/83)

Pray and abandon your hearts to me, because I wish to be with you. (12/12/83)

What is most important for your body is prayer. (12/22/83)

My children, pray, pray, pray. Remember that the most important thing in our lives is prayer. (12/27/83)

When others cause you some difficulty, do not defend yourself; rather, pray. (-/-/83)

Without prayer you cannot do anything. (01/19/84)

Do not give up on meditation. (01/21/84)

You have not understood well what it means to pray. May you understand that; I desire it very much. (01/23/84)

Pray much. I desire that you be saturated with prayer. (01/24/84)

You need vigour in your prayer. May you pray for a long time in meditation, and fervently. (01/25/84)

I wish that you always deepen your life in prayer. Every morning say the Prayer of Consecration to the Heart of Mary. Do it in a family. Recite each morning the Angelus, the Lord's Prayer, the Hail Mary, and the Glory Be five times in honour of the Holy Passion, and a

91

sixth time for our Holy Father, the Pope. Then say the Creed and the Prayer to the Holy Spirit; and, if possible, it would be well to pray one part of the Rosary. (01/27/84)

Pray! I desire to purify your hearts. Pray. It is indispensable, because God gives you the greatest graces when you pray. (01/30/84)

Do not think of anything else except of those for whom you pray. [E.g., when praying for sinners and unbelievers.] Then prayer will be better and you will be faithful to it. (01/31/84)

With prayer, your body and soul will find peace. (02/04/84)

When I say, "Pray, pray, pray," I do not mean to just increase the number of hours of prayer, but also to reinforce the desire for prayer, and to be in contact with God. Place yourself permanently in a spiritual state bathed in prayer. (06/26/84)

Today I wish to tell you: always pray before your work, and end your work with prayer. If you do that, God will bless you and your work. These days you have not been praying much but working a lot; therefore, pray. In prayer, you will find rest. (07/05/84)

In prayer abandon yourselves to God. (08/09/84)

In every prayer you must listen to the voice of God. (09/10/84)

Today I want to tell you that you make me happy again and again by your prayer, but there are enough of those in this very parish who do not pray, and my heart is saddened. (10/04/84)

Prayer is a conversation with God. To pray means to listen to God. Prayer is useful for you because after prayer everything is clear. Prayer makes one know happiness. Prayer can teach you how to cry. Prayer can teach you how to blossom. Prayer is not a joke. Prayer is a dialogue with God. (10/20/84)

Do not ask yourself the reason why I constantly invite you to prayer. Intensify your personal prayer so that it will become a channel for others. (11/17/84)

Your days will not be the same according to whether or not you pray. (-/-/84)

Be patient and constant in your prayers. (01/14/85)

I do not need the Lord's Prayer said a hundred or two hundred times. It is better to pray only one, but with a desire to encounter God. (03/09/85)

In prayer you will discover the greatest joy and the way out of every situation that has no escape. (03/28/85)

Today I call you to prayer with the heart, and not just from habit. (05/02/85)

Sometimes prayers said in a loud voice keep Jesus at a distance, because when people want to conquer with their own strength there is no place for God. Prayers said out loud are good when they come from the heart. (05/03/85)

Every prayer which comes from the heart is agreeable to God. (-/-/85)

Let prayer, dear children, be your everyday food, especially when your work in the fields is wearing you out so much that you cannot pray with the heart. Pray, and then you will overcome even every weariness. Prayer will be your joy and your rest. (05/30/85)

One has to be prepared ahead of time. If there are some sins, one must uproot them, otherwise one will not be able to enter into prayer. If there are concerns, they should be submitted to God. (-/03/85)

I beseech you, dear children, approach prayer consciously. In prayer you will come to know God's greatness. (11/28/85)

If you pray with the heart, dear children, the ice of your brothers' hearts will melt, and every barrier will disappear. Conversion will be easy for all who desire to accept it. This is the gift which you must obtain by prayer for your neighbour. (01/23/86)

Every second of prayer is like a drop of dew in the morning which refreshes fully each flower, each blade of grass, and the whole earth. In the same way prayer refreshes everyone. When a person is tired he will get rest; when he is troubled he will find peace again. He is renewed, and can once again listen to the words of God... Temptations, which come on him again and again, make him weak, and he needs to always get from prayer a new power for love, and freshness. (01/27/86)

Dear children, I beseech you to open yourselves and begin to pray. Prayer will be your joy. If you make a start, it will not be boring for you because you will be praying out of joy. (03/20/86)

Pray for the gift of love, for the gift of faith, for the gift of prayer, for the gift of fasting. (04/17/86)

Without prayer, dear children, you cannot experience either God, or me, or the graces which I am giving you. Therefore, my call to you is that the beginning and end of your day always be prayer. Dear children, I wish to lead you daily more and more in prayer, but you are not able to grow because you do not desire it. My call, dear children, is that for you prayer be in the first place. (07/03/86)

Dear children, my call to you is that your prayer be the joy of an encounter with the Lord. I am not able to guide you as long as you yourselves do not experience joy in prayer! From day to day I desire to lead you more and more in prayer, but I do not wish to force you. (08/14/86)

I am calling you, so that by your prayer and your life you help to destroy everything that is evil in people and uncover the deception that Satan makes use of. Pray that the truth prevails in all hearts. (09/25/86)

If you want to love, pray for your brothers and sisters. Today many people need lots of prayers. Pray, and be a model to others because through you I want to lead people towards the light. (-/-/-)

Dear children, you cannot understand how great the value of prayer is as long as you yourselves do not say, "Now is the time for prayer; now nothing else is important to me; now not one person is important to me except God." Dear children, consecrate yourselves to prayer with special love so that God will be able to bestow graces on you. (10/02/86)

Not with words, but rather through prayer, will you attain what you desire. (10/06/86)

I am calling you to prayer and complete surrender to God, because Satan wants to sift you through everyday affairs and in your life he wants to snatch the first place. Therefore, dear children, pray without ceasing! (10/16/86)

Especially, dear children, do I call you to pray for peace. Without your prayers, dear children, I cannot help you to fulfill the message which the Lord has given me to give you. Therefore, dear children, pray so that in prayer you realize what God is giving you. (10/23/86)

When you pray you are much more beautiful, like flowers which, after the snow, display all their beauty, and all their colours become indescribable. So also, dear children, after prayer you will show more strongly before God everything that is beautiful; this pleases him. Therefore, dear children, pray, and open your inner self to the Lord so that he may make of you a harmonious and beautiful flower for Paradise. (12/18/86)

All your prayers touch me very much, especially your daily Rosary. (-/-/87)

Therefore, dear children, pray, and in prayer you will realize a new way of joy. (02/25/87)

You know, dear children, that God grants special graces in prayer... So pray that God's blessing may protect each one of you from all the evil that is threatening you. (04/25/87)

Continue to pray in spite of everything and you will understand the will of the Father, and his love. (05/16/87)

Create in your hearts a permanent prayer, because only thus will you be able to be prepared vessels. (07/11/87)

Prayer is the only way to save the human race. (07/30/87)

Let prayer be your life. Dear children, dedicate your time only to Jesus and he will give you everything that you are seeking. He will reveal himself to you in fullness. (09/25/87)

Pray, because in prayer each one of you will be able to achieve complete love. (10/25/87)

Dear children, Satan is very strong. And therefore I request your prayers – that you offer them for those who are under his influence that they be saved… If you pray, Satan cannot injure you, not even a little, because you are God's children and He is watching over you. Pray, and let the Rosary always be in your hands as a sign to Satan that you belong to me. (02/25/88)

Pray now for people who curse against the name of God. (04/11/88)

Do not pray just with your lips, but pray with the heart. In this way prayer will obtain victory! (07/04/88)

God is offering himself and giving himself to you. But he seeks from you that you answer his call freely. Therefore, little children, set a time during the day when you can pray in peace and humility and meet with God the Creator. (11/25/88)

I invite you to pray, and to ask me boldly for graces. I will intercede for you before God. (01/19/89)

Little children, at all times fill your heart with even the smallest prayers. (02/25/89)

Dear children, this is a time of grace. Pray as much as you can and renew yourselves through prayer. Build yourselves up spiritually. This building up lasts until the end of your lives. (03/27/89)

Pray, because you are under great temptation and danger; the world and material goods lead you into slavery. Satan is active in this plan. I want to help each one of you in prayer. (06/25/89)

Through prayer you are richer in the mercy of God. Therefore, little children, let prayer be light for each one of you. Especially, I call you to pray so that all those who are far from God may be converted. Then our hearts will be richer because God will rule in the hearts of all people. Therefore, little children, pray, pray, pray. Let prayer begin to reign in the whole world. (08/25/89)

Tonight especially, I want to ask you to give me your problems and difficulties so that you can pray with more freedom and more joy - so that your prayer becomes a prayer with the heart. (05/11/90)

I do not desire that you talk about prayer, but that you pray. Let your days be filled with prayers of gratitude to God for life and for all that you have. (04/25/91)

Pray, my dear little children, so that prayer becomes your daily bread. (01/25/92)

Pray for peace, because Satan wants to destroy the little peace you have. (06/25/92)

Little children, decide for prayer. Only in this way will you be happy, and God will give you what you seek from him. (12/25/93)

It is only through prayer that we can defeat evil and protect all that Satan wants to destroy in your life. (02/25/94)

Dear children, today I invite you to decide to give time patiently for prayer... Little children, do not forget that if you do not pray, you are not close to me, nor are you close to the Holy Spirit who leads you along the path to holiness. (07/25/94)

Let prayer be life for you. (08/25/95)

I wish, dear children, that during this time you find a corner for personal prayer. I want to lead you towards prayer with the heart. Only in this way will you comprehend that your life is empty without prayer. You will discover the meaning of your life when you discover God in prayer. (07/25/97)

Only with prayer, dear children, will your heart change, become better, and be more sensitive to the Word of God. (01/25/98)

Today, little children, I invite you, through prayer, to be with Jesus, so that from a personal experience of prayer you may be able to discover the beauty of God's creatures. You cannot speak or witness about prayer if you do not pray. That is why, little children, in the silence of the heart, remain with Jesus so that he may change and transform you with his love. (07/25/98)

Today I invite you to come still closer to me through prayer. Little children, I am your Mother, I love you, and I want each of you to be saved and thus be with me in Heaven. That is why, little children, pray, pray, pray, until your life becomes prayer. (08/25/98)

In a special way, little children, I call you to pray for the conversion of sinners, for those who pierce my heart and the heart of my Son Jesus with the sword of hatred and daily blasphemies. Let us pray, little children, for all those who do not wish to come to know the love of God, even though they are in the Church. Let us pray that they convert so that the Church may resurrect in love. (03/25/99)

Little children, be strong and pray so that prayer may give you strength and joy. (06/25/99)

It is only through prayer that you will become my apostles of peace in this restless world. (11/25/99)

I call you, little children, to pray without ceasing. If you pray, you are closer to God and he will lead you on the way to peace and salvation. (01/25/2000)

Pray in a special way for those who do not know God's love; and witness with your life so that they can also come to know God and his immeasurable love. (02/25/2000)

Little children, pray without ceasing, until prayer becomes joy for you. (03/25/2000)

I call you to prayer so that through prayer you put God in the first place. (11/25/2000)

This is a time of grace. Therefore pray, pray, pray until you comprehend God's love for each of you. (02/25/2001)

Little children, prayer works miracles. (04/25/2001)

And you, do not be afraid because the one who prays is not afraid of evil and has no hatred in his heart. (09/25/2001)

I am with you and I thank God for each of you who has accepted and live prayer with seriousness. (10/25/2001)

Open yourselves to prayer so that prayer becomes a need for you. (02/25/2002)

PRAYER GROUPS

Communities of prayer are needed in all parishes. (04/11/82)

If you pray, a source of life will flow from your hearts. If you pray with strength, if you pray with faith, you will receive graces from this source, and your group will be strengthened. (10/24/83)

Renew prayer in your families and form prayer groups. In this way, you will experience joy in prayer and togetherness. All those who pray and are members of prayer groups are open to God's will in their hearts and joyfully witness God's love. (09/25/2000)

PRIESTS

You have asked me to keep good and faithful priests in this parish who will continue the work. Do not be afraid of anything. This grace will be given to you.

I do not demand anything from priests other than prayer with perseverance and preaching. May they be patient and wait for the promise of God. (06/23/82)

Yes, it is better that the children pray with me and that the pilgrims ask the priests and look for solutions with them. (12/20/82)

Priests should visit families, more particularly those who do not practise anymore and who have forgotten God. Priests should carry the Gospel of Jesus to the people and teach them how to pray. Priests themselves should pray more, and also fast. They should give to the poor what they do not need. (05/30/84)

Let all priests pray the Rosary. (06/25/85)

I ask you to pray in a special way for Pope John Paul II and for priests. (07/10/92)

PURGATORY

There are many souls in Purgatory, including persons who have been consecrated to God – some priests, some religious. For their intentions pray at least the Lord's Prayer, the Hail Mary, and the Glory Be seven times each, and the Creed. I recommend it to you. There is a large number of souls who have been in Purgatory for a long time because no one prays for them. (07/21/82)

These persons wait for your prayers and your sacrifices. (-/-/83)

In Purgatory there are different levels; the lowest is close to Hell and the highest gradually draws near to Heaven. It is not on All Souls Day, but at Christmas, that the greatest number of souls leave Purgatory. In Purgatory there are souls who pray ardently to God, but for whom no relative or friend prays on earth. God lets them benefit from the prayers of other people. It does happen that God permits them to manifest themselves in different ways, close to their relatives on earth, in order to remind people of the existence of Purgatory and to solicit their prayers to come near to God who is just, but good. The majority of people go to Purgatory. Many go to Hell. A small number go directly to Heaven. (01/10/83)

Today I wish to call you to pray daily for the souls in Purgatory. (Prayer and grace are necessary for every soul to reach God and his love.) And, in this way, dear children, you obtain new intercessors who will help you in life to realize that all earthly things are not important for you, that Heaven is the only goal for which it is necessary to strive. Therefore, dear children, pray without ceasing that you may be able to help yourselves and others to whom your prayers will bring joy. (11/06/86)

QUEEN OF PEACE FEAST DAY

I would prefer that it take place on June 25th. The faithful came for the first time on that day, on the hill. (02/02/82)

June 25th should be celebrated as the Feast of Mary, Queen of Peace. (06/-/84)

RECONCILIATION

My Son suffers very much because men do not want to be reconciled. They have not listened to me. Be converted, be reconciled. (10/15/83)

Be reconciled, because I desire reconciliation among you, with more love for each other, like brothers. I wish that prayer, peace, and love bloom in you. (02/02/84)

Today I wish to call all of you to Confession, even if you have confessed a few days ago. I wish that all of you experience my feast day within yourselves. But you cannot experience it unless you abandon yourselves completely to God. Therefore, I am inviting all of you to reconciliation with God. (03/24/85)

You should consecrate three days to reconciliation each month: the first Friday of the month, followed by Saturday and Sunday. (-/-/85)

REINCARNATION

It is false to teach people that you are reborn many times and that you pass to different bodies. A person is born only once. The body, drawn from the earth, decomposes after death. It never comes back to life again. A person receives a transfigured body. (07/24/82)

RELIGIONS

Members of all faiths are equal before God. God rules over each faith just like a sovereign over his kingdom. In the world, not all religions are the same because not all people have complied with the commandments of God. They reject and disparage them. (10/01/81)

Tell this priest, tell everyone, that it is you who are divided on earth. The Muslims and the Orthodox, for the same reason as Catholics, are equal before my Son and me. You are all my children. Certainly, not all religions are equal, but all people are equal before God, as St. Paul says. It does not suffice to belong to the Catholic Church to be saved, but it is necessary to respect the commandments of God in following one's conscience.

Those who are not Catholics are no less creatures made in the image of God, and their destination is someday to rejoin the House of the Father. Salvation is available to everyone without exception. Only those who deliberately reject God are condemned. To him who has been given little, little will be asked for; to him who has been given much, very much will be required. It is God alone, in his infinite justice, who determines the degree of responsibility and pronounces judgment. (-/-/84)

RENUNCIATION

Renounce all passions and all inordinate desires. Avoid television, particularly evil programs, excessive sports, unreasonable enjoyment of food and drink, alcohol, tobacco, etc. (06/16/83)

In this season I especially want you to renounce all the things to which you are attached but are hurting your spiritual life. (02/25/90)

Today in a special way I invite you all to prayer and renunciation. For now as never before Satan wants to show the world his shameful face by which he wants to seduce as many people as possible onto the way of death and sin. Therefore, dear children, help my Immaculate Heart to triumph in the sinful world. I beseech all of you to offer prayers and sacrifices for my intentions so I can present them to God for what is most necessary. Forget your desires, dear children, and pray for what God wants, and not for what you want. (09/25/91)

In a special way I call you to renunciation in this time of grace. Little children, through your little sacrifices meditate on and live the passion and death of Jesus which he endured for each one of you. It is only by coming closer to Jesus that you will comprehend the immeasurable love he has for each of you. Through prayer and renunciation you will become more open to the gift of faith and love towards the Church and the people who are around you. (02/25/98)

Also today I call you to fasting and renunciation. Little children, renounce everything that hinders you from being closer to Jesus. In a special way I call you: pray, because only through prayer will you be able to overcome your will and discover the will of God even in the smallest things. (03/25/98)

ROSARY

The Rosary is not an ornament for the home, as one oftentimes limits oneself to using it in this way. Tell everyone to pray it. (03/18/85)

I urge you to ask everyone to pray the Rosary. With the Rosary you will overcome all the troubles which Satan is trying to inflict on the Catholic Church. Let all priests pray the Rosary. Give time to the Rosary. (06/25/85)

Advance against Satan by means of prayer. Satan wants to work even more now that you know he is at work. Dear children, put on the armour for battle and, with the Rosary in your hand, defeat him! (08/08/85)

Let the faithful meditate each day on the life of Jesus while praying the Rosary. (-/-/85)

Today I call you to begin praying the Rosary with a living faith. That way I will be able to help you. Dear children, you wish to obtain graces, but you are not praying. I cannot help you because you do not want to get started. Dear children, I call you to pray the Rosary and to let this be a task you fulfill with joy. (06/12/86)

I wish only that for you the Rosary become your life. (08/04/86)

All your prayers touch me very much, especially your daily Rosary. (-/-/87)

The Rosary alone can already work miracles in the world and in your lives. (01/25/91)

Pray all three mysteries of the Rosary daily for non-believers. (03/18/91)

Dear children, in this time I call you to pray the Rosary in your family. (08/14/92)

I call all priests and religious brothers and sisters to pray the Rosary and to teach others to pray. The Rosary, little children, is especially dear to me. Through the Rosary open your heart to me, and I can help you. (08/25/97)

When you are tired and sick, and you do not know the meaning of your life, take the Rosary and pray; pray until prayer becomes for you a joyful meeting with your Saviour. (04/25/2001)

RUSSIA

The Russian people will be the people who will glorify God the most. (10/-/81)

SACRAMENTS

Strengthen your faith through prayer and the sacraments. (08/08/81)

It is necessary to believe firmly, to go to Confession regularly, and likewise to receive Holy Communion. (02/10/82)

SACRIFICES

I thank you for every sacrifice you have offered. And now I urge you to offer every sacrifice with love. (07/04/85)

And offer your sacrifices to Jesus in order that everything is fulfilled the way he has planned it and that Satan can accomplish nothing. (01/09/86)

I wish to thank you for all the sacrifices, and I invite you to the greatest sacrifice, the sacrifice of love. (03/27/86)

I ask that during the next three days each of you make a sacrifice, giving up something that is dear to you in life. (08/11/89)

The prayers and sacrifices you decided to offer in the days when I asked you were not done with love. I ask you to offer them with love as you did during the first days of my apparitions. What you decided to do and to offer for my intentions during the novena was not enough. You have to choose to give more because you are capable. (12/18/89)

I need your prayers and sacrifices for peace. (01/11/91)

Today again I thank you for all that you have accomplished for me in these days. Especially, dear children, I thank you in the name of Jesus for the sacrifices which you offered during this past week. Dear children, you forget that I want sacrifices from you so that I can help you and drive Satan away from you. Therefore, I am calling you again to offer sacrifices with a special reverence toward God. (09/18/96)

Dear children, today I call you to prepare yourselves, through prayer and sacrifice, for the coming of the Holy Spirit. (05/25/98)

SAINTS

The important thing is to pray to the Holy Spirit so that he may descend on you. When one has him, one has everything. People make a mistake when they turn only to the saints to request something. (10/21/83)

I wish you to be a beautiful bouquet of flowers which I desire to present to God for the feast day of All Saints. I invite you to open yourselves and to live with the saints as your examples. Mother Church has chosen them that they may be an impetus for your daily life. (10/25/94)

SATAN

A great struggle is about to unfold, a struggle between my Son and Satan. Human souls are at stake. (08/02/81)

Excuse me for this, but you must realize that Satan exists. One day he appeared before the throne of God and asked permission to submit the Church to a period of trial. God gave him permission to try the Church for one century. This century is under the power of the devil, but when the secrets confided to you come to pass, his strength will be destroyed. Even now he is beginning to lose his power and has become aggressive. He is destroying marriages, creating division among priests and is responsible for obsessions and murder. You must protect yourselves against these things through fasting and prayer, especially community prayer. Carry blessed objects with you. Put them in your house, and restore the use of holy water. (11/-/81)

The devil is trying to conquer us. Do not permit him. Keep the faith, fast, and pray. I will be with you at every step. (11/16/81)

Do not let the enemy take possession of you in anything. Be courageous. (02/11/82)

Satan exists! He seeks only to destroy. (02/14/82)

Satan says only what he wants. He interferes in everything. My angels, be ready to endure everything. Many things will take place here [in Medjugorje]. Do not allow yourselves to be surprised by him. (02/16/82)

Be prudent, because the devil tempts all those who have made a resolution to consecrate themselves to God – most particularly those people. He will suggest to them that they are praying too much, that they are fasting too much, that they must be like other young people and go in search of pleasures. Tell them not to listen to him or obey him. It is to the voice of the Blessed Virgin that they should pay attention. When they are strengthened in their faith, the devil will no longer be able to seduce them. (06/16/83)

If you would be strong in faith, Satan would not be able to do anything against you. (04/05/84)

Dear children, these days Satan wants to frustrate my plans. Pray that his plan will not be realized. I will pray to my Son Jesus to give you the grace to experience His victory over the temptations of Satan. (07/12/84)

Do not permit Satan to take away your courage. (01/14/85)

Satan wants to work still more fiercely to take away the joy from each one of you. By prayer you can completely disarm him and ensure your happiness. (01/24/85)

Satan wants to impose hardships on the Catholic Church. (06/25/85)

Do not be afraid of Satan. That is not worth the trouble, because with humble prayer and an ardent love, one can disarm him. (08/-/85)

Satan wants to work still more now that you know he is at work. Dear children, put on the armour for battle and, with the Rosary in your hand, defeat him! (08/08/85)

Dear children, do not allow Satan to take control of your hearts so that you become an image of him and not of me. (01/30/86)

Dear children, Satan is lurking around each individual. Especially in everyday affairs he wants to spread confusion among you. Therefore, dear children, my call to you is that your day would only be prayer and complete surrender to God. (09/04/86)

Wherever I appear, and wherever my Son comes with me, there Satan also comes. (01/28/87)

Satan is strong and is waiting to test each one of you. Pray, and that way he will neither be able to injure you nor block you on the way of holiness. (09/25/87)

I want you to obey me and not permit Satan to seduce you. Dear children, Satan is very strong. And therefore I request your prayers - that you offer them for those who are under his influence that they be saved... If you pray, Satan cannot injure you, not even a little, because you are God's children and He is watching over you. Pray, and let the Rosary always be in your hands as a sign to Satan that you belong to me. (02/25/88)

Dear children, today again your Mother wishes to warn you that Satan, by every means possible, desires to ruin everything in you; but your prayers prevent him from succeeding. When you fill up all the empty spaces with prayer, you prevent Satan from entering your soul. (03/21/88)

I am your Mother and I caution you that this is a time of temptation. Satan is trying to find emptiness in you so that he can enter and destroy you. DO NOT SURRENDER! I pray with you. Do not pray just with your lips, but pray with the heart. In this way prayer will obtain victory! (07/04/88)

A little spiritual emptiness in you is enough for Satan to work in you. For this reason your Mother invites you to begin to pray. May your weapon be prayer. With prayer of the heart you will overcome Satan. (09/05/88)

Satan wants, in this time, to be active through your weakness. This is why, dear children, your Mother invites you: pray, pray, pray. Do not allow Satan to enter. Close all the entrances. Prayer is the best weapon. (07/13/90)

Satan is strong and wishes not only to destroy human life but also nature and the planet on which you live. Therefore, dear children, pray that you can protect yourselves through prayer with the blessing of God's peace. God sent me to you so that I can help you. If you wish, grasp the Rosary. The Rosary alone can already work miracles in the world, and in your lives. (01/25/91)

I am with you also in these restless days in which Satan wants to destroy everything that I and my Son Jesus are building up. In a special way he wants to destroy your souls. He wants to guide you as far away as possible from Christian life and from the commandments which the Church is calling you to live. Satan wants to destroy everything that is holy in you and around you. Therefore, little children, pray, pray, pray, in order to be able to comprehend all that God is giving you through my coming here. (09/25/92)

Dear children, at this time Satan wishes to act through small, small things, dear children. Therefore, pray! (10/02/92)

I am your Mother, little children, and I do not want Satan to deceive you, for he wants to lead you the wrong way. But he cannot if you do not permit him. (07/25/93)

In this time, Satan wants to create disorder in your hearts and in your families. Little children, do not give in. You must not permit him to lead you and your life. (01/25/94)

It is only through prayer that we can defeat evil and protect all that Satan wants to destroy in your life. (02/25/94)

Satan is strong and with all his forces wants to bring the most people possible closer to himself and to sin. That is why he is on the prowl to snatch more every moment. I beg you, little children, pray and help me to help you. (05/25/95)

Satan wants to destroy the family. The family is in crisis. Pray. (06/25/95)

Little children, do not permit Satan to pull you apart and to do what he wants with you. (01/25/98)

Pray, dear children, particularly in this period, when Satan is trying to destroy your families. (09/20/99)

SECRETS

Concerning the secrets, my children, these are not known by the people. But when they will learn of them, it will be too late. Return to prayer! There is nothing more important! I dearly wish that the Lord would permit me to enlighten you a little more on these secrets, but the grace which is offered to you is already great enough. (01/28/87)

SIGN

My sweet angels, even if I were to leave the sign, many people would still not believe. Many will only come here and bow down. But people must be converted and do penance. (07/21/81)

The sign will be given at the end of the apparitions. Hurry to be converted. Do not wait for the great sign. For the unbelievers, it will then be too late to be converted. (09/04/81)

You are not to ask me any more questions on the subject of the sign. Do not be afraid, it will surely appear. I carry out my promises. As far as you are concerned, pray, and persevere in prayer. (10/26/81)

The sign will appear at the right time. (01/21/82)

The great sign has been granted. It will appear independently of the conversion of the people. (08/31/82)

Beforehand, several warnings will be given to the world. (04/25/83)

The sign will come, you must not worry about it. The only thing that I would want to tell you is to be converted. Make that known to all my children as quickly as possible. (06/24/83)

SIMPLICITY

If you want to be very happy, live a simple, humble life, pray a great deal, do not delve into your problems, but let yourselves be guided by God.

Do not complicate matters. Yes, you can walk on a deeper spiritual level but you will have difficulties. Take the simple way. (-/-/84)

In simplicity, each of you will become like a child who is open to the love of the Father. (07/25/96)

SIN

My clothes were sparkling. Behold them soaked with tears. Oh, if you only knew how the world is plunged into sin today. It may seem to you that the world does not sin any longer, because here you live in a peaceful world where there is neither confusion nor perversity.

If you only knew how lukewarm they are in their faith, how many do not listen to Jesus, oh, oh, if you only knew how much I suffer, you would sin no more. (11/06/83)

The world has been drawn into a great whirlpool. It does not know what it is doing. It does not realize into what sin it is sinking. It needs your prayers so that I can pull it out of this danger. (02/17/84)

There are so many who live in sin. There are likewise some among you here who have offended my heart. Pray and fast for them. (03/21/84)

Many times, confronting justice and confronting your sins, many times I returned from your home in tears. I could not say a single word. I am your Mother and I do not want to oppose you. But what I will do in you is up to you. (04/24/84)

Please, do not let my heart weep with tears of blood because of the souls who are being lost in sin. Therefore, dear children, pray, pray, pray! (05/24/84)

Pray still more these days for the conversion of sinners. (08/02/84)

Look around you, dear children, and you will see how greatly sin has dominated the world. Pray, therefore, that Jesus conquers. (09/13/84)

Dear children, all the prayers which you recite in the evening in your homes, dedicate them to the conversion of sinners because the world is immersed in a great moral decay. (10/08/84)

If you wanted to accept my love, you would never sin. (10/-/85)

I want each one of you to be happy, but with sin nobody can be happy. (02/25/87)

You are ready to commit sin and, without thinking, put yourselves in the hands of Satan. (05/25/87)

SPECIAL BLESSING

Today I am blessing you with the Solemn Blessing that the Almighty grants me. (08/15/85)

Bless [with the Special Blessing] even those who do not believe. You can give them this Blessing from the heart, to help them in their conversion. Bless everyone you meet. I give you a special grace. I want you to give this grace to others. (11/29/88)

Today I am giving you my Special Blessing. Carry it to every creature so that each one may have peace. (12/25/88)

STRENGTH

I wish to strengthen you, but prayer alone is your strength. (12/30/83)

Pray and fast, so that during this novena God will fill you with his strength. (03/17/84)

I give you strength, dear children; with this strength you can endure everything. (06/27/88)

I will give you strength, and I will help you in all your needs. You can ask for everything that you need to help you. I will intercede for you before God. (11/23/88)

Your Mother will help you and she will give you the strength to continue. (12/25/89)

SUFFERING

The cross is necessary because of the sins of the world. (Spring/82)

So when sufferings come, offer them up as a sacrifice to God. (03/29/84)

By means of the cross, God is glorified through every person. (11/29/84)

Prayer for a sick person

O my God,
behold this sick person before you;
he has come to ask you for what he wants
and for what he considers most important for him.
O my God,
please make these words enter into his heart:
"What is important is the health of his soul."
Lord, may your will in everything be done in his regard.
If you want him to be cured
let health be given to him;
but if your will is something else
let him continue to bear his cross.
I also pray to you for us
who are interceding for him;
purify our hearts
so as to make us worthy
to convey your holy mercy.
Protect him and relieve his pain
so that your holy will be done in him,
and so that your holy name be revealed through him.
Help him to bear his cross with courage.
(06/22/85)

Especially, dear children, pray that you may be able to
accept sickness, and sufferings with love – the way Jesus
accepted them [sufferings]. Only in that way will I be
able, with joy, to give out to you the graces and healings
which Jesus is permitting me. (09/11/86)

Dear children, I want to invite you, under this cross, to
take your cross as the will of God. As my Son took up

his cross, so you must carry everything, and my Son will be glorified through your crosses. (03/29/91)

When you are sick, when you suffer from something, do not say, "Oh, why has this happened to me and not to somebody else?" No, say instead, "Lord, I thank you for the gift you are giving me." For sufferings are really great gifts from God. They are sources of great graces for you and for others. When you are sick, many of you only pray and repeat, "Heal me, heal me." No, dear children, this is not correct because your hearts are not open; you shut your hearts through your sickness. You cannot be open to the will of God or to the graces he wants to give you. Pray this way: "Lord, thy will be done in me." Only then can God communicate his graces to you according to your real needs which he knows better than you. It can be healing, new strength, new joy, new peace. Just open your hearts. (11/-/91)

I am with you and your suffering is also mine. (04/25/92)

Today I invite you to offer your crosses and suffering for my intentions. Little children, I am your Mother and I wish to help you by seeking graces for you from God. Little children, offer your sufferings as a gift to God so that they may become a most beautiful flower of joy. Therefore, little children, pray that you may understand that suffering can become joy, and the cross the way of joy. (09/25/96)

When you are tired and sick and you do not know the meaning of your life, take the Rosary and pray; pray until prayer becomes for you a joyful meeting with your

Saviour. I am with you, little children, and I intercede and pray for you. (04/25/2001)

TELEVISION

It would be a good thing to give up television because, after seeing some programs, you are distracted and cannot pray. (12/08/81)

If you watch television programs, if you read the newspapers, your heads are filled with news, then there is no longer any place for me in you hearts. (04/17/86)

THANKSGIVING

Pray also in the evening when you have finished your day. Sit down in your room and say to Jesus, "Thank you." (10/30/83)

It is raining at this time and you say, "It is unreasonable to go to church in this mud. Why is it raining so much?" Do not ever speak like that. You did not stop praying that God would send you rain which makes the earth rich. Then do not turn against the blessing from God. Above all, thank him through prayer and fasting. (02/01/84)

Dear children, learn to give thanks in little things and then you will be able to give thanks also for the big things. (10/03/85)

Little children, give thanks unceasingly for all that you possess, for each little gift which God has given you, so that a joyful blessing always comes down from God upon your life. (08/25/88)

I would like you to thank God for your family, for the place where you work, and for the people God puts in your path. (08/29/88)

Little children, rejoice in everything that you have, and give thanks to God because everything is God's gift to you. That way you will be able to give thanks for everything in your life and discover God in everything, even in the smallest flower. (04/25/89)

Today I invite you to give thanks to God for all the gifts you have discovered in the course of your life, and even for the least gift you have received. I give thanks with you, and I want all of you to experience the joy of these gifts. (09/25/89)

In thanking him you will discover the Most High and all the good things that surround you. Little children, God is great, and his love for every creature is great. Therefore, pray to be able to understand the love and goodness of God. (10/25/95)

Dear children, thank my Son for all the graces that he has given you. (06/25/99)

I call all of you, little children, to give thanks to God here with me for the graces which he gives you through me. (07/25/99)

TIME OF GRACE

Dear children, this is a time for grace. That is why I would like you to pray as much as you can during this time. Especially, I would like you to renew family prayer. (11/07/88)

This is a time of grace. Little children, today in a special way with little Jesus whom I hold in my embrace, I am giving you the possibility of deciding for peace. Through your 'Yes' for peace and your decision for God, a new possibility for peace is opened to you. Only in this way, little children, will this century be for you a time of peace and well-being. (12/25/99)

Wake up from the sleep of unbelief and sin, because this is a time of grace which God gives you. Use this time, and seek from God the grace of healing of your heart so that you may see God and people with the heart. (02/25/2000)

I rejoice with you, and in this time of grace I call you to spiritual renewal. (05/25/2000)

At this time of grace, I call you to prayer. Little children, you work much but without God's blessing. Bless and seek the wisdom of the Holy Spirit to lead you at this time so that you may comprehend and live in the grace of this time. Convert, little children, and kneel in the silence of your hearts. Put God at the centre of your being so that, in this way, you can witness in joy the beauty that God continually gives in your life. (05/25/2001)

Little children, make good use of this time of grace…" (06/25/2001)

In this time of grace, I call you to come even closer to God through your personal prayer. (07/25/2001)

TRIALS

You will be subjected to trials, but you will bear them with great ease. We will be ready to show you how to escape from them if you accept us. (04/15/84 – Holy Week)

At this moment my Son's gift and mine is this: you will be comforted in your trials. They will be easier for you because we will be close to you. If you listen to us, we will show you how to overcome them. (04/21/84)

These days you have been experiencing how Satan is working. I am always with you; so do not be afraid of trials because God is always watching over us. I have also given myself to you, and I empathize with you even in the smallest trial. (07/19/84)

Be assured, dear children, that God tests you because he loves you. Always offer up all your burdens to God and do not be anxious. (10/11/84)

Give me all your feelings and all your problems! I wish to comfort you in all your trials. I wish to fill you with peace, joy, and the love of God. (06/20/85)

Today I wish to tell you that God wants to send you trials which you can overcome by prayer. God is testing you through daily chores. Pray now to withstand every trial in peace. From everything by which God tests you come out more open to God; and approach him with love. (08/22/85)

In difficulties, when you are carrying the cross, sing; be full of joy. (-/-/86)

UNBELIEVERS

Hurry to be converted. Do not wait for the great sign. For the unbelievers it will be too late to be converted. (12/15/82)

How very large are the numbers of unbelievers! That will change only if you help me with your prayers. (02/09/84)

My angel, pray for unbelievers. People will tear their hair, brothers will plead with brothers, they will curse their past lives which were lived without God. They will repent, but it will be too late. Now is the time for conversion. (08/15/85)

For those who say, "I do not believe in God," how difficult it will be when they approach the Throne of God and hear the voice: "Enter into Hell." (10/08/85)

They [unbelievers] are my children. I suffer because of them. They do not know what awaits them. You must pray more for them. (10/25/85)

Once more I beseech all of you to pray, and help unbelievers by your prayers. They do not have the grace to experience God in their hearts with a living faith... I want to tell you how I suffer for all because I am the Mother of all. (03/18/89)

Do not impose your faith on unbelievers. Show it to them by your example, and pray for them. My children, pray! (02/02/90)

Pray all three mysteries of the Rosary daily for nonbelievers, and attend Mass especially for them once a month. God knows what their needs are; they must bring them to him personally. (03/18/91)

UNION WITH GOD AND WITH MOTHER MARY

I wish that your hearts will be united to mine, as my heart is united to that of my Son. (03/30/84)

Today it is not words or deeds which are important. The important thing is only to pray, to remain in God. (09/-/86)

When you find union with God, you will feel hunger for the kingdom of God, and your hearts, little children, will overflow with joy. You will witness God's love wherever you are. (01/25/97)

123

Today I call you to let your life become united with God the Creator, because only in this way will your life have meaning, and you will understand that God is love. (04/25/97)

VISIONARIES
The most important thing is that you, the visionaries, remain united. Let peace be among you. Pay very close attention to that. Obey and do what the priests and your parents tell you. Go often to Mass and receive Communion. Be very attentive these days. Some dishonest people will come to you in numbers, in order to tempt you. Be careful of your statements. These days I expect of you a very special discipline. Do not move around anywhere, or often, and do not separate from one another.

A number of those who have been very enthusiastic will cool off. But you, persist and be appreciative of each of my words. (06/23/82)

I know that many will not believe you, and that many who have an impassioned faith will cool off. Remain firm, and persuade people immediately to prayer, penance and conversion.

In the end, you will be happier. When you suffer difficulties and need anything, come to me. (-/-/83)

WAR
The third world war will not take place. (07/12/82)

Through fasting and prayer one can stop wars, one can suspend the laws of nature. (07/21/82)

Also today, I call you to prayer, especially today when Satan wants war and hatred. I call you anew, little children: pray and fast that God may give you peace. Witness peace to every heart and be carriers of peace in this world without peace. I am with you and intercede before God for each of you. And you, do not be afraid because the one who prays is not afraid of evil and has no hatred in his heart. (09/25/2001)

WARNINGS
Be converted! It will be too late when the sign comes. Beforehand, several warnings will be given to the world. Hurry to be converted. (04/25/83)

WEST, THE
The West has made progress in civilization, but without God, as if they were their own creators. (10/-/81)

Monthly Confession will be a remedy for the Church in the West. One must convey this message to the West. (08/06/82)

WHO DOES OUR LADY SAY SHE IS?
I am the Blessed Virgin Mary. (06/26/81)

I am the Mother of God and the Queen of Peace. (10/12/81)

I am the Queen of Peace, and I am also your Mother. Do not forget that I am your Mother and I love you. (01/02/2000)

WHY DID OUR LADY CHOOSE MEDJUGORJE?
I have come because there are many true believers here. (06/26/81)

Dear children, this parish which I have chosen, is special and different from others. And I give great graces to all who pray with the heart. (02/06/86)

WHY IS OUR LADY APPEARING ON EARTH AT THIS TIME?

I wish to be with you to convert and to reconcile the whole world. (06/26/81)

I have come to call the world to conversion for the last time. Afterwards, I will not appear anymore on this earth. (05/02/82)

I have come to tell the world that God is truth; he exists. True happiness and fullness of life are in him. I have come here as Queen of Peace to tell the world that peace is necessary for the salvation of the world. In God, one finds true joy from which true peace is derived. (06/16/83)

I call on each one of you to consciously decide for God and against Satan. I am your Mother and, therefore, I want to lead you all to complete holiness. I want each one of you to be happy here on earth and to be with me in Heaven. Dear children, that is the purpose of my coming here, and it is my desire. (05/25/87)

My presence here is therefore to lead you on a new path, the path of salvation. Thus I call you day after day to conversion, but if you do not pray you cannot say you are converting. (06/25/92)

Dear children, these times are special, and therefore I am with you to love and protect you, to protect your hearts from Satan and to bring you all closer to the heart of my Son Jesus. (06/25/93)

Out of love for people, God has sent me among you to show you the path of salvation, the path of love. (04/25/95)

God sends me to you out of love, that I may help you to comprehend that without him there is no future or joy, and above all, there is no eternal salvation. Little children, I call you to leave sin and to accept prayer at all times, that in prayer you may come to know the meaning of your live. (04/25/97)

WHY IS OUR LADY REMAINING
SO LONG?

I have stayed with you this long so that I may help you along in your trials. (02/07/85)

Today I am calling you to reflect upon why I am with you this long. (07/17/86)

The fact that I am with you for such a long time is a sign that I love you immeasurably. (10/09/86)

Dear children, it is for your sake that I have stayed this long so I can help you carry out all the messages which I am giving you. Therefore, dear children, for love of me, put into practice all the instructions which I am giving you. (10/30/86)

Dear children, you know that for your sake I have remained a long time so that I may teach you how to make progress on the way of holiness. Therefore, dear children, pray without ceasing, and live the messages which I am giving you, for I am doing it with great love toward God and toward you. (01/01/87)

Dear children, this is the reason for my presence among you for such a long time: to lead you on the path of Jesus. I want to save you and, through you, the whole world. (07/30/87)

WITNESS

Carry my messages with humility, in such a way that on seeing happiness in you, people will want to be like you. (07/-/85)

Love. If you do not love, you cannot transmit the testimony. You cannot witness either for me or for Jesus. (06/06/86)

Be a reflection of Jesus. This way, you will be his witnesses in your lives. But you cannot be his reflection without prayer. (02/15/88)

Give witness by your life; sacrifice your lives for the salvation of the world. (02/25/88)

God gave you the gift of holiness. Pray that you may understand it more and more, and in that way you will be able to bear witness for God by your life. (09/25/88)

I call every one of you to live the messages I give, and to witness by your lives. (01/16/89)

Pray that you may be open to everything that God is doing through you. (01/25/89)

I invite you to become apostles of love and goodness. In this world without peace, give witness to God and his love, and God will bless you and give you what you seek of him. (10/25/93)

Little children, I wish that all people convert and see me and my Son Jesus in you. I will intercede for you and help you to become light. (05/25/96)

Especially, I call all those who have consecrated themselves to my Immaculate Heart to become an example to others. (08/25/97)

Little children, I desire for you to become carriers of peace and of God's joy to today's peace-less world. (10/25/97)

Little children, I have led you and am still leading you through this time of grace so that you may become conscious of your Christian vocation. Holy martyrs died witnessing: "I am a Christian, and I love God above everything else." Little children, today I also invite you to rejoice, and be joyful Christians, responsible and conscious that God called you in a special way to be joyfully extended hands toward those who do not believe, and that through the example of your life, they may receive faith and love for God. (11/25/97)

Pray in a special way for those who do not know God's love, and witness with your life so that they can also come to know God and his immeasurable love. (02/25/2000)

Little children, you are chosen to witness peace and joy. (10/25/2001)

Pray for peace in your hearts and work for your personal conversion. Little children, only in this way will you be able to become witnesses of peace and of the love of Jesus in the world. Open yourselves to prayer so that prayer becomes a need for you. Be converted, little children, and work so that as many souls as possible may come to know Jesus and his love. (02/25/2002)

WORK FOR GOD AND HIS CHURCH

Do now everything you can so that the world may be converted. (06/01/83)

Today I wish to call you to work in the Church. I love all of you equally, and I desire from each one of you to work as much as possible. I know, dear children, that you can but you do not wish to, because you feel small and humble in these matters. You need to be courageous, and with little flowers do your share for the Church and for Jesus so that everyone can be happy. (10/31/85)

I wish that each of you decide for a change of life and that each of you work more in the Church, not through words and thoughts but through example, so that your life may be a joyful testimony for Jesus. (02/25/93)

Little children, I also wish that all of you become active during this time which is connected to Heaven through me in a special way. Pray in order to understand that all of you, through your life and your example, ought to collaborate in the work of salvation. (05/25/96)

Today I invite you in a special way to open yourselves to God the Creator and to become active. I invite you, little children, to see at this time who needs your spiritual or material help. By your example, little children, you will be the extended hands of God which humanity is seeking. Only in this way will you understand that you are called to witness and to become joyful carriers of God's word and love. (02/25/97)

I wish to thank you and to inspire you to work even more for God and his kingdom with love and with the power of the Holy Spirit. (08/25/2000)

WORKS OF MERCY

Let everyone get up early, some to go to school, others to work, still others to help the poor like themselves, and also to help those who need assistance. (01/18/84)

Continue to help the poor, the sick, and to pray for the dead. (01/31/84)

Do not look with scorn on those who beg you for a piece of bread. Do not turn them away from your full tables. Help them, and God will also help you. Perhaps it is in this way that God will hear you, and the blessing that he wants to give you in gratitude will be realized. (01/28/87)

I call each one of you to begin to live as of today the life which God wishes of you, and to begin to perform good works of love and mercy. (03/25/87)

Today I invite you to do works of mercy with love, and out of love for me and for our brothers and sisters, yours and mine. (11/25/90)

YOUNG PEOPLE

Tell the young people not to allow themselves to be distracted from the true path. Let them remain faithful to their religion. (10/30/81)

Dear children, today I call you to renew prayer in your families. Dear children, encourage the very young to prayer, and encourage the children to go to Mass. (03/07/85)

I wish especially to say to the young people: be open to the Holy Spirit because God wants to draw you to himself in these days when Satan is at work. (05/16/85)

Especially, I wish to call the youth of the parish. They are dear to me. (10/10/85)

Dear children, you are forgetting that you are all important. The elderly are especially important in the family. Urge them to pray. Let all the young people be an example to others by their lives, and let them witness to Jesus. Dear children, I beseech you, begin to change through prayer and you will know what you need to do. (04/24/86)

Young people find themselves now in a very difficult situation. Help each other. I think about you in a special way, dear children. Young people have a role to play in the Church now. Pray, dear children. (08/15/88)

Dear children, I would like to tell you tonight, during these days pray especially for the young. I would like to recommend to "my" priests to create and organize groups where young people are taught and given good counselling for their lives. You, dear children, who are present tonight, you must be the messengers of the Good Word of peace to others, especially to young people. (08/22/88)

Dear children, tonight also, your Mother is warning that Satan is at work. I would like you to pay particular attention to the fact that Satan is at work in a special way against the young. Dear children, during this period I would like you to pray in your families with your children. I would like you to talk with your children. I would like you to exchange your experiences and help them to solve all their problems. I will pray, dear children, for the young, and for all of you. Pray, dear children. Prayer is medicine that heals. (09/09/88)

Dear children, your Mother wants to call you to pray for the young of the whole world and for the parents of the whole world that they will know how to educate their children and how to lead them in life with good advice. Pray, dear children; the situation of the young is difficult. Help them! Help parents who do not know, who give bad advice! (10/24/88)

In the future I would like to see parents work and pray as much as they can with their children in the families, so that they can strengthen their spirit from day to day. (08/14/89)

Dear children, I again ask you to pray for all the young people of the world because they find themselves in a difficult situation. You can help them with your love and prayers of the heart. (-/-/89)

Dear children, today I call you to decide for God during these days. You, young people, put God first in your lives. With him you will have a way that is sure. (08/02/92)

I am with you, and I teach you, little children: your peace and hope are in God. Therefore, draw closer to God and put him in the first place in your life. Thank you for having responded to my call. (01/25/2001)

SONGS OF MEDJUGORJE

The first hymn is an English version of the composition by the former choirmaster of St. James' Church in Medjugorje, the late Fra Stanko Vasilj. He introduced the Croatian words and music to the parish on the 30th of August 1981, two months after Our Lady's first apparitions in Bijakovici on the east end of Medjugorje. He lovingly called this tiny village Bijakovo.

This translation is faithful to the original; it is idiomatic, and possibly the most singable of all the existing English renditions. The correct title is *MAJCI I KRALJICI MIRA*, *TO THE MOTHER AND QUEEN OF PEACE*.

Permission is hereby granted to anyone who wishes to use this translation in public, provided the following credit is cited. "Composer in the Croatian language: Fra Stanko Vasilj. Translator into English: Andrew Jerome Yeung."

The words of the second hymn, *TO THE QUEEN OF PEACE OF MEDJUGORJE*, is based on the main messages of Our Lady. The lyrics were first written in Croatian and flow much better in that language than in this translation. Please instruct singers that the last syllable of "Medjugorje" is pronounced like the "ye" in "year" (which rhymes with "there").

The famous melody is by the Austrian Catholic composer Franz Lehar. He died over 50 years ago, and the tune is therefore free for use in North America. But it is not so in Europe and some other countries. Please check and obtain written permission before utilizing.

To Our Mother and Queen of Peace

1. We have come to you, dear Mo-ther,
2. All the Church is look-ing to you
3. Bi-ja-ko-vo, your wee ham-let,
4. For the to-tal love, dear Mo-ther,

1. from all cor-ners of this pla-net.
2. as a lode-star of sal-va-tion.
3. and the whole of Me-dju-gor-je
4. which you've poured out here up-on us,

1. bring-ing you our heart-aches burn-ing,
2. Cleanse us, Mo-ther and em-brace us;
3. spread your mes-sage and your glo-ry,
4. we now pledge you our en-dea-vour

and in them our deep-est yearn-ing.
hear our voi-ces beg you grace us.
praise your name and tell your sto-ry.
to be bet-ter more than ev-er.

Majci i Kraljici Mira
Composer: Fra Stanko Vasilj
Translator: Andrew Jerome Yeung
Translation Copyright © 2001

To The Queen Of Peace Of Medjugorje

Franz Lehar (1870-1948)
Andrew Yeung (1938 -)

Largo

1. To you Queen of Peace, our joy- ful
2. We give you our pledge to of- ten
3. Mo- ther Ma- ry, we've re- spon- ded

prais- es sing,
go to Mass,
to your call

With tre- men- dous love our fi- lial
And to pray with fer- vent hearts, and
To live peace to which your mes- sage

hon- our bring.
glad- ly us
bids all.

Blest a- mong all wo- men
To be- lieve God firm- ly,
Thank you for the grace of

and e- ter- nal- ly
and our sins con- fess,
Med- ju- go- rj- e;

Dear- est in our hearts, Our La- dy,
To do pen- ance and con- vert in
Thanks for gift of peace and ap- pa-

you will be;
ho- li- ness.
ri- tions there.

OTHER BOOKS BY ANDREW JEROME YEUNG

Do Whatever Jesus Tells You!

The Way to Medjugorje.

Parents, Peace!

The Rosary (A Worried Parent Prays).

The Fruitful Servant – A seminar in preparation for productive Christian service. Candidates' Booklet.

The Fruitful Servant – A seminar in preparation for productive Christian service. Team Manual.

All are available at:

The Ave Maria Centre of Peace
P.O. Box 489, Station U
Toronto, Ontario, M8Z 5Y8
Canada